MACBYRD

MACBYRD
OR A MISCHIEF OF MAGPIES

PETE TALBOT

Copyright © 2017 Pete Talbot

The moral right of the author has been asserted.

Apart from any fair dealing for the purposes of research or private study, or criticism or review, as permitted under the Copyright, Designs and Patents Act 1988, this publication may only be reproduced, stored or transmitted, in any form or by any means, with the prior permission in writing of the publishers, or in the case of reprographic reproduction in accordance with the terms of licences issued by the Copyright Licensing Agency. Enquiries concerning reproduction outside those terms should be sent to the publishers.

Amateur and professional performing rights

Applications for performance, and also readings where admission charges are to be made, should be addressed to

The Rude Mechanical Theatre Company,
The Peppe Nappa Studio,
Unit 8 Commercial Mews,
42A Commercial Road,
Eastbourne BN21 3XF,
or by email to therudes@btinternet.com. 01323-501260.

No performance of any kind may be given unless a licence has been obtained.
Applications should be made before rehearsals begin.

Matador
9 Priory Business Park,
Wistow Road, Kibworth Beauchamp,
Leicestershire. LE8 0RX
Tel: 0116 279 2299
Email: books@troubador.co.uk
Web: www.troubador.co.uk/matador
Twitter: @matadorbooks

ISBN 978 1788037 273

British Library Cataloguing in Publication Data.
A catalogue record for this book is available from the British Library.

Printed and bound in the UK by TJ International, Padstow, Cornwall
Typeset in 11pt Minion Pro by Troubador Publishing Ltd, Leicester, UK

Matador is an imprint of Troubador Publishing Ltd

For Sue

AUTHOR'S NOTE

For a long time people have been asking for scripts of the plays performed by The Rudes, or they have said, 'Why don't you film them?' It is, of course, a great compliment that people should want to 'preserve' them and I am genuinely pleased. However, the term suggests pickling or jam making – as if we might be able to take them out of the cupboard from time to time at our whim and have another helping. Of course, I am being flippant; I know that people have genuinely enjoyed them and want in some way to continue the experience. But let us consider what 'Macbyrd' is, or, I should say, was.

It was a piece of theatre (performed outdoors fifty or so times in the summer of 2016 on village greens, primary school playing fields, recreation grounds, and the like, around the South of England) – and what is theatre? It is an event that happens at a particular time in an agreed meeting place where actors and audience come together and share in the performance of a story. Yes, of course, it happens on the stage, but it also happens – and primarily perhaps – in the audience's minds.

They agree to listen and have their attention diverted from this point to that point around the stage as the action unfolds and carries them from the beginning, with the setting out of principles and ground rules about how it is to be done, to the end when the various strands of the story come together – and, the key point, it happens there and then, with that particular assemblage of minds, beliefs and expectations of what theatre is brought to that event by the audience, actors and playwright and shared together.

You could even say it happens there and then fifty or more times, for us each summer, each time being subtly different from the previous. There is, of course, a pre-theatre (the script, the rehearsals, what the audience already know about the play, or don't know about it) and an after-theatre (what they take away with them, the memories, the discussion in the bar, the programme), but the play itself once the actors leave the stage is over. It exists only for that period of time, that precious period of time when, hopefully, the magic takes place and the story is played out – and you were either there, or you weren't.

What is contained in this volume, therefore, is a record, a memory, a shadow of a play when the actors have left the stage – and, of course, as that it does have a function. What I hope this volume will do is let you experience the story again in a different format which, we hope, will be enjoyable and help you remember what the original piece of theatre was like – and encourage you to come and see us again making other pieces of theatre. In some respects it is important that 'Macbyrd' is preserved, if you value it at all that is, because it happened like all our plays – and like all rural touring – on the outposts of the theatre industry where the critics do not come and where reputations are rarely made. But good things aren't only made in the bright lights of cities and the theatrical shrines of the West End.

HOW MACBYRD WAS MADE

It began as a script but not a conventional script. I always begin with a series of canovacci, usually about twenty. Much of this terminology by the way comes from the commedia dell'arte. (See below the section on the importance of commedia to our work.) Each canovaccio (translated literally as a canvas, or note pad) is made up of one or more scenes, or series of events, maybe a number of gags, sometimes physical gags which we call lazzi, songs, dances sometimes, mimes, and a range of styles of speech. These may be battute, when short bits of text are batted backwards and forwards in strict time, or they may be 'rich text' like poems or set speeches. The actors mess with these at their peril! Or it may be simple dialogue. One key element is all'improvviso. This is marked as such in the script and consists of recommended text in parentheses, which is fluid and can be altered at will by the actors, but usually settles down through rehearsals. It is especially important for complex mimes, like the rescue of Hugo from the crashed spitfire, because working out the action has to be done first and then the text fitted in around it.

Plans for all this are set out in so many canovacci (twenty in Macbyrd's case), which taken together are called the scenario. This forms the skeleton or underlying structure around which the play is made. A lot of thinking, planning, speculative text, possible gags, and so on, goes into constructing the scenario – and then a proto-script (or working script) is written and used in rehearsals.

Because it is multiple role-playing (There are usually six actor/musicians in our plays and occasionally an extra non-speaking stage manager/musician) I often make costume changes impossible. This isn't because of a sadistic tendency on my part. When we know how long an actor needs to change we create 'bridge passages', either of further script or action, or music, so that he or she has time to get back on as another character. This creates the illusion that there are far more actors than there actually are (and keeps the wage bill down). Sometimes once the play is on the road there is opportunistic all'improvviso when actors react to something in the audience and speak off the cuff. The play is a much less fixed entity than more conventional plays, therefore, often changing from night to night, and another reason why it cannot be pinned down in a simple script like this.

COMMEDIA DELL'ARTE

The theatre genre called the commedia dell'arte – our single most important influence – first flourished in Italy in the 16th century and was performed by the first professional troupes of actors. It then spread throughout Europe during the 17th and 18th centuries. The most famous characters were Harlequin, Colombine, the doctor and the bombastic captain, Il Capitano. Its influence on a whole range of artistic forms from panto to silent movie, from opera to classical ballet, has been enormous. It has been especially influential in our work. It is not the function of this introduction to discuss in detail what commedia is and isn't, but there are things which it is not for us and things which it definitely is for us.

For example we have never, or rarely, used its stock characters. We make our own characters relevant to English audiences *in the manner of* the commedia dell'arte, using archetypes and developing their 'whole body' movement in the commedia way using the 'vertical axis' and animal models where appropriate. In Macbyrd especially, but in most of our plays, we use English archetypes like Gertie or PC Wood or Cygnus (rather than the typically Italian ones of the tradition). We do not freely improvise the whole play. Not that commedia even did at the height of its great flourishing. There were always set speeches and pre-written passages of battute and sproloquio (flowery bombastic speech), for example, in 'commonplace books' which the actors used as 'scripts'; we do use all'improvviso, however, as explained above.

In Macbyrd we don't use much slapstick, nor the battoccio or wooden slapstick, although we often do in other plays. We will never be pinned down by the tradition. We do what the play demands, not the tradition. And we don't use leather masks. But even in the tradition not all characters wore leather masks. Some, like us, used white face (or pantomime blanche) – and we do that because the leather masks are a very Italian thing, while in England white face is more familiar through circus. But all the 'masks' – and by the 'mask' we are talking about the whole character, the white face or leather mask, the wig-hats, the posture, gesture, gait and clown-like costume – have the key role of 'cartoonising' the character, that is, we are telling the audience that the actors aren't trying to copy people walking down the street, but are figures (archetypes essentially) in a story. It's just storytelling.

We also use mime – not in any stylised way like Marcel Marceau – but, as children do, to keep the story flowing and not get bogged down in scenery and physical objects. We supplement this with vocal sound effects (vsfx in the script) to stimulate the imagination. Why have a real door when the sound of a door is more interesting?

Essentially, therefore, we use commedia dell'arte as we need it. Our main aim is to create relevant stories for contemporary audiences. The San Francisco Mime Troupe famously wanted to create a new kind of physical theatre which spoke for the 20th century and found that the commedia dell'arte had already done it.

MACBYRD

We have created sixteen brand new plays for the Rudes, so why publish 'Macbyrd' in particular? Well to begin with we hope to publish them all in time, but this one has been among the most popular, so based on your feedback we have started with 'Macbyrd'.

The play (along with 'Gentle Harry's Farm', to which it is related) deals with the relationship between middle class conventional society and 'the outsiders' who apparently threaten our values. This theme is taken up in both stories, that of the 'oomans and of the birds. In the case of the 'ooman story it is the real upstart Hitler who threatens the settled life of the village, but also the perceived threat of gypsies, fifth columnists and black marketers. Among the birds it is the working class upstart raven, Macbyrd, who challenges and destroys the swan, symbol of the monarchy and the moneyed classes, the threat of the dispossessed 'rising up', but also 'foreigners' in the form of the Indian bush lark – and of course the 'gypsy magpies' are also there being a general nuisance.

Change is the problem, or perceived change; we don't want our settled order to be messed with by 'outsiders'. How do we deal with it? Is it for good or evil? Commedia has always been about the struggle between the powerful and the dispossessed. Not that we take a political position. One thing I have learnt as a Left winger working in a 'conservative' part of the country is that the important thing is not to tell people what we think they should believe. That is insulting. But rather to seek for and appeal to the humanity in people whatever their political views – and there is humanity across the political divide.

'Macbyrd' is rather a political play, but in the broad sense of how we, in our largely middle class comfortable world, deal with change when we appear to be threatened by outsiders. It turned out to be particularly poignant in 2016 with Brexit and its anxiety about 'foreigners'. To quote from the programme: 'Are these things frightening, or are they just change? Is it a nettle we have to grasp, or a new world? I guess in the end the play comes down in favour of the bravery of keeping one's own standards of decency, just carrying on, the heroism of ordinariness, Lil's and George's kind of heroism, and an admiration of those who when it comes to it step up, like Wilf, and do the right thing.'

But then hopefully you will know all this already because you were there when the play happened.

Pete Talbot

MACBYRD

Jevington, Sussex – June 1940

CHARACTERS

THE 'OOMANS

GEORGE BEESKEP
A retired garage mechanic
– *Pall Palsson*

WILF BEESKEP
His son. A garage mechanic
– *André Refig*

BRIONY SHAWCRISS
A young woman seeking love.
Runs the dramatic society
– *Miriam Swainsbury*

**WING-COMMANDER
HUGO FFINCH-HATTON**
Billeted in the village
– *Pall Palsson*

MRS DORA PENTLOW
Runs the WI
– *Miriam Swainsbury*

LIL BEESKEP
His wife. Runs the post office
– *Georgie Field*

JACK BANNISTER
The cricket captain
– *Chris Lindon*

GERTIE GORDON
Her friend & daughter of the
village doctor
– *Georgie Field*

BIFFY
An airman
– *Huw Blainey*

PC ALF WOOD
The village policeman
– *Huw Blainey*

CEDRIC LILYWHITE
A man from the ministry
– *Chris Lindon*

THE BIRDS

MACBYRD
A raven & mayor of Aviana
– Chris Lindon

WORMWOOD
A raven. His wife
– Georgie Field

CYGNUS
A swan. Supreme Leader of Aviana
– Pall Palsson

PEN
A swan. His consort
– Miriam Swainsbury

QUILL
A goose & bureaucrat in Macbyrd's office
– Huw Blainey

FEATHER
A heron. Another bureaucrat
– André Refig

INSPECTOR SEED
A pigeon & detective
– Pall Palsson

THORN
A magpie
– André Refig

NIGHTSHADE
A magpie
– Huw Blainey

YEWBERRY
A magpie
– Miriam Swainsbury

PROFESSOR BHATTACHARJEE
An Indian bushlark
– Huw Blainey

Jennifer
A poor wren
– Georgie Field

ROSEBUD
A busybody old maid of a coot
– Georgie Field

BERTHA
Her sister
– Miriam Swainsbury

PETER
A poor sparrow
– André Refig

PEGOTTY
His wife
– Georgie Field

and...
Al 'Twist' Clark
MUSICIAN & STAGE MANAGER

THE PRODUCTION TEAM

Costumes
– Kim Bishop, Annette Keen, Anna Styliannou
& Caroline Tully

Birds' heads
– Kim Lapworth

Poster design
– Gill Toft

Pageant wagon painting
– Pennie & Alan Radcliffe, and Rob Watson

Web site
– Clive Gross

Front of House
– Glenn Overington with the Friends & many local teams

Choreography by The team lead by *Georgie Field*

Music composed, arranged & directed
by *Rowan Talbot*

WRITTEN AND DIRECTED BY PETE TALBOT

MACBYRD

CANO 1

THE LETTER – *Hillside Cottage, Jevington, under the Downs. A hot sunny morning. June 1940. The garden.*
Thorn (M1), George Beeskep (M2), Nightshade (M4), Yewberry (F1) & Lil Beeskep (F2)

Music 1 – 'The Magpie Song'

> *Thorn flies in. His manner is sinister and aggressive. Squawks menacingly at the audience. Settles & smokes a cigarette. All'improvviso magpie noises (Chark! Chark! Ch-ch-ch-ch! Etc).*

> *Yewberry flies in with a chick in her beak chased by Nightshade. She tries to avoid him.*

NIGHTSHADE   Chick! Chick! Chick! Chick! Gimme the chick! Gimme the chick!
YEWBERRY   *(They struggle over the chick.)* I will not! Chark! Chark!
THORN   Nightshade! Yewberry! *(They go into music hall mode.)*

1

Why do yuh always have to fight?
You won't go hungry now the chickidies are ripe.
For their mothers like to feed 'em
'Til they're fat an' plump an' sweet – an'
They always make a very tasty bite.
(To the audience.) To eat our kind, you see, is just what magpies do.
We're not moved when we hear a sparrow mew.
When we peck its bones for marrow
For us it doesn't harrow.
It's merely food – a dish, a snack, a stew.

THORN, YEWBERRY & NIGHTSHADE
For the magpie is a very simple bird.
Any other thought is unquestionably absurd.
For us it's black or white;
No such thing as wrong or right;
Of morality, per se, we've never heard.
A swallow will merely wallow in its charm.
A blackbird ever rarely cause alarm.
A mute swan will never moot
A censure or law suit,
And a chaffinch will hardly ever do you harm
And a skylark never irritates or narks.

They'll sing in rain, in sunshine, or when dark.
She'll gently feed her babies
Among buttercups and daisies.
(Slowing down) But the magpie will simply eat the lark.

Music 1 – ends

THORN	*(Fierce.)* Listen! The wind 'as changed. Listen to the leaves. *(They simultaneously take a drag on cigarettes as they listen to the leaves.)*
THE OTHERS	*(They listen to the wind.)* Chaaaark.
LIL	*(Off.)* I'll bring it out, George.
THORN	*(Alert suddenly.)* Quiet! *(Pause.)* 'Oomans!
YEWBERRY	Chark!
THORN	Yewberry! *(She caws submissively. Pause. They freeze. George enters whistling. He has a garden fork. Nightshade & Yewberry fly out, but Thorn circles & returns.)*

Lil enters with a cup of tea, a piece of cake and a letter on a tray.

GEORGE	*(Calls off to Lil.)* Got some a' tha' cake, Lil? *(Digs up cabbages, which he admires. To the audience.)* Look at tha'! Cabbages for a king, ay. Ne'er mind the

	war effort.
LIL	Cuppa tea an' a piece a'cake!
GEORGE	Nice cuppa 'fore I gets started. They wunt complain o'er my coffin if you supply the grub. *(To the audience.)* Queen of upside down cake, she is. In't yuh Lil? *(Eats.)*
LIL	*(She shrieks with laughter.)* Listen to 'im! I'll die a'fore you do, you leathery ol' boot, you! *(He laughs.)*
THORN	Ch-ch-ch-ch! Chark! Chark! *(Yewberry & Nightshade return. They chatter.)*
GEORGE	Listen t'those birds! I'll tell yuh, they in't nothin' lovelier than the Downs in a stinkin' 'ot June with the little birds twittering innocently away. *(The magpies hold an evil looking tableau for a few seconds smoking.)*
LIL	Oh. Chap on a motorbike brought this. Look. *(Stares at the envelope.)* It says 'Secret. To be opened only by George Beeskep'. *(Shows him. He takes it.)*
GEORGE	What's this then? *(Puts his glasses on. Reads the envelope.)* 'The War Office'.

Thorn listens, head cocked on one side. The others chatter imitating George ('What's this then? This then!' Etc.) & search for snicketies.

> It's from The War Office! *(Anxious.)* I 'ope I in't bin called up.

LIL	Called up at your age! Don't be daft! Mr Churchill in't that desperate.
GEORGE	*(Studying the letter.)* Wha's this? Wha's this?

Music 2 – begins

MAGPIES	Chark! Ch-ch-ch-ch! Ch-ch-ch-ch! What's this! What's this!
LIL	What is it, George?

Music 2 – ends

GEORGE	I gotta go up t'London! Urgently!
LIL	Wha'? No! Surely….
GEORGE	I 'ave! It say, 'For the attention of Mr George Beeskep. I 'ereby give you notice tha' you are required under the War Measures Act, 1st day of September, 1939, to attend for interview as soon as possible with myself…' Err, let's see. *(Turns the letter over.)* 'Cedric…' *(Pronounces it See-dric.)*
LIL	*(Corrects him.)* Cedric.
GEORGE	'Cedric… Lilywhite.' 'Oo the 'ell's 'e? 'In Room 736, The War Office, 'Orseguards Avenue, London.'
LIL	It's a mistake! Surely?
GEORGE	'And… you should note that this is a ma'er of absolute secrecy. You are advised tha' you should not speak of

	this to anyone and if you do you may be charged under the Treachery Act, 23rd day of May, 1940, which may carry a prison sentence. Signed Cedric Lilywhite, Esq.' *(He stares at her in shock.)*
LIL	Oh, George! *(They cling to each other.)* Wha' can it be?
GEORGE	But what d' they wants me for? *(To the audience.)* I in't nothin' but a retired ol' mo'or mechanic diggin' vegetables for the war effort! *(To Lil.)* I in't done nothin'.
LIL	They knows tha'. *(Smiles. Very positive. Almost excited.)* Well, I think you mus' be impor'ant in some way. Tha's wha' I think!
GEORGE	*(Smiles importantly at the audience.)* Impor'ant? D'yuh think so?

Vsfx & double bass. Bombers, ours, begin to pass overhead, their engines humming.

LIL	I does!
GEORGE	P'raps I'd be'er go now then? *(Takes his watch out.)* There's a train from Polegate Station at five past 8. I'll get a ticket. I can be in London by 10.00.
LIL	*(Urgent.)* You'll need your suit! I'll go and press it. *(Leaves to go into the house.)*

GEORGE	I'd be'er get the Enfield out. I 'ope there's enough petrol t'get me t'the station.
LIL	*(She stops and turns round smiling broadly.)* Well, 'oo d've thought! *(To the audience.)* My 'usband. Called up t'the War Office! I'm proud of you, George Beeskep. You're an important man.
GEORGE	*(Tableau of personal pride.)* D'yuh think so?
LIL	I does. *(Gives him a hug and exits indoors.)*
GEORGE	*(The humming gets louder. He & the magpies look up.)* Bombers. Ours. *(Pause.)* 'Ummin' like a million bees. Good luck, boys. *(Turns and goes into the house as the humming fades.)*

Music 3 – begins

CANO 2

A MURDER OF MAGPIES – *The same*

Thorn (M1), Macbyrd (M3), Nightshade (M4), & Yewberry (F1)

MAGPIES	*(The magpies gather round conspiratorially.)* Chark! Ch-ch-ch-ch! Ch-ch-ch-ch! What's this! What's this!
THORN	*(Looking up into the sky.)* A raven flew as the sun crept low
THE OTHERS	*(Whisper.)* Peck out 'is eyes! Peck out 'is eyes!
THORN	*(To the audience.)* To a brook where a swan swam all alone
THE OTHERS	*(Whisper.)* Peck out 'is eyes! Peck out 'is eyes!
THORN	And lay his neck on the swan's white down And pressed his beak with a silent moan 'Til blood like jewels fell all around.
THE OTHERS	*(Whisper.)* Peck out 'is eyes! Peck out 'is eyes!

A raven, Macbyrd, flies in, black, and sleek as silk, and lands nearby on a branch, head held high and wings outstretched, bouncing like a tight-rope walker.

	Macbyrd!
THORN	Maaarrkk! Macbyrd.
MACBYRD	Kark! Kark! What is it Thorn? You don' worry me, you chick-stealers, dancin'

	and prancin' on yuh twiggy legs!
THORN	Macbyrd, with your raven's silky coat and black as night beak, your time has come. *(He lowers his body subserviently. The others follow.)* Listen to the wind.
MACBYRD	What! Kark! Kark! What time an' gypsy charm is this, magpies? Time for you t'steal sparrars' eggs, no doubt! *(The magpies chatter malevolently.)*
NIGHTSHADE	Listen to the wind, Macbyrd!
YEWBERRY	The wind 'as changed! Can't you 'ear?
MACBYRD	*(Begins to fly away.)* So the wind 'as changed yuh mischief-makers!
THORN	*(Bows. Sarcastic.)* My lord, Macbyrd!
THE OTHERS	*(They bow, too.)* My lord, Macbyrd!
MACBYRD	Wha'! Kark! I ain't no lord. What's this? *(They echo the phrase in whispers.)* I'm a clerk, tha's all! *(To the audience)* An 'umble artisan, that's me, with claws as rough as oak, who 'as become mayor of Aviana – where birds rule, not 'oomans – *(To the magpies)* through 'ard work! And loyalty. Tha's all I am! *(Checks his watch.)* An' I've work t'do, so I'll be… *(About to fly.)*
THORN	*(Stops him.)* But second only to one!
MACBYRD	What? *(Thoughtful.)* The jewelled swan! *(Forceful again.)* Ch-ch-ch-ch! Ch-ch-ch-ch! Maaarrk! *(To the audience)* Who rules the brook, the lake an' the water meadows an' always will! *(To the*

	magpies.) An' what is that to you?
NIGHTSHADE	Lord of all an' lord of none.
MACBYRD	Don' give me yuh poisonous berries, Nightshade.
YEWBERRY	Second to one, but lord of all, Macbyrd.
MACBYRD	Pretty as a flower… *(Hard)* but just as deadly, Yewberry!
THORN	*(Looking up into the sky.)* A raven flew as the sun crept low…
MACBYRD	What! Wha' are these riddles? Kark!
THE OTHERS	*(Whisper.)* Peck out 'is eyes! Peck out 'is eyes!
THORN	To a brook where a swan swam all alone…
MACBYRD	Ch-ch-ch! Enough of this mischief! *(Macbyrd screeches & chatters refusing to listen.)*
THORN	And lay his neck on the swan's white down
YEWBERRY	An' pressed 'is beak with a silent moan
NIGHTSHADE	'Til blood like jewels fell all around.
MACBYRD	Blood?
THE OTHERS	*(Whisper.)* Peck out 'is eyes! Peck out 'is eyes!
THORN	Your time has come, Macbyrd! The day of the swan is finally done. And the stream's frantic race through the vale is run; Brook will be hay and fields become clay Just as the night will follow the day.

	(Looks at the audience.) 'Oomans will march all over the green
	and feet will run where lake has been.
	Dark winged birds will rule meadow an' rye
	Sleek an' shiny an' black against sky!
MACBYRD	What! Kark! Be gone you devils!
YEWBERRY	Give 'im the raven's kiss, Macbyrd!
MACBYRD	*(Turns on her savagely.)* I will not! *(She & Nightshade fly off screeching.)*
THORN	Listen, Macbyrd!
	And the swan lay down by the worried brook
	An' cried aloud to choughs an' rooks.
	What do this mean? What's this? What's this?
	'A raven's kiss. That's all. Just this.'
MACBYRD	I will not listen! Kark!
THORN	*(Screeches.)* Listen!
	'Ah! A kiss,' said the swan. 'So you love me still.'
	An' the raven sighed, 'I do an' I will.'
	An' they wrapped their necks like lovers will
	An' lay by the nest breathing hard until
	The sun painted red the vale an' the hill.

MACBYRD	*(Thorn makes to go. Macbyrd pursues him.)* Wha's this mean, Thorn? Wha' are these riddles? Kark!
THORN	Your time has come, Macbyrd!
GEORGE	*(Off.)* I'll be away then, Lil
THORN	'Oomans! *(Flies out.)*
MACBYRD	*(Calls after him.)* Thorn! Wha' is this mischief? *(To the audience.)* They make promises which ain't promises an' raise 'opes which ain't 'opes! What does it mean 'a raven's kiss' an' 'blood fell all around'? I'm loyal! I am! An 'umble servant. An' always will be. *(George pushes in his Enfield; Lil is with him holding a bag. He's in his best suit.)* Kark! Ch-ch-ch-ch!

CANO 3

George goes to London & Wilf is recruited – *The street near Hillside Cottage.*
Wilf Beeskep (M1), George (M2), Jack Bannister (M3), Briony Shawcriss (F1), Lil Beeskep & Gertie Gordon (F2)

Music 3 – ends

LIL	It's lovely to 'ear the birds, in't it! They're so cheerful. *(Macbyrd karks, then flies off.)* It makes you feel good to be alive! Now, George. I've packed you some sandwiches an' some upside down cake.
GEORGE	Oo, tha's good. *(To the audience.)* I like upside down cake. *(Putting on his gauntlets.)* Thank you, Lil. D'yuh think I'll see the king?
LIL	You might. You'll prob'ly see Mr Churchill at least. Off yuh go an' remember, don' tell no-one where yuh goin'. Yuh know wha' the le'er say. Don' want no bobbies arrestin' you now. With a bit'a luck nobody munt notice you.
WILF	*(Enters. Notices George's suit immediately.)* 'Ello Pop. Where you 'arf
LIL	to? I sees yuh've got your suit on. 'E in't goin' nowhere, so mind yuh business.
WILF	*(To the audience.)* Well, I only axed 'im, tha's all.

GEORGE	I 'spec yuh'll all talk o'er my grave in the same way.
LIL	Go on with yuh. *(George kick starts his Enfield. Vsfx.)*
WILF	Ay, Pop. Tha' Austin Seven tha' come in, Dr Gordon's, gonna need a new big end an' we in't got none in.
LIL	Now, no time t'talk garage talk today. Your pa 'as t'go to London.
WILF	*(To the audience.)* Well, I only mentioned…
GEORGE	*(Firm.)* Lil! *(Whispers.)* Yuh know wha' the letter said.
LIL	Ooops! *(Puts her hand over her mouth.)*
WILF	Sounds like sommat *is* goin' arf t'me.
LIL	Nothin' in't goin arf 'cept your Pop an' 'e 'as a train t' catch, so… *(Kisses him goodbye)* we'll be seein' you later.
WILF	Well, I only…
GEORGE	Alright. Ta-ta.
LIL	Take care now! Arf you go. *(She waves as he rides off.)*
WILF	*(Looks at her questioningly.)* Ma! Wha'…?
LIL	In't you got no work t'do, young man? They'll be queueing up down there. *(Goes in.)*
WILF	Ma! *(To himself.)* Well, I only axed!
BRIONY	*(Briony Shawcriss enters cheerfully.)* I say, Wilf. Just the chep I wanted to see. By the way *(Looking off)*, was thet your

	pater I saw in a suit? I wonder where he's orf to. *(To the audience.)* Mystery in abundance, what?
WILF	Mornin' Briony. *(Sighs.)* Wha' do you want then?
BRIONY	*(She grabs his arm. He's very uncomfortable.)* Horrors maximus! Gerald Collington has jacked in the drama society outdoor Macbeth so I need someone to play Macduff rather end I thought ol' Wilf is just the ticket.
WILF	Bu' wha' about Jack... *(Eases his arm out),* your boyfriend? 'E's much better'n...
BRIONY	Oh, Jack's playing Macbeth, 'course. The ol' thing kent do both! *(To the audience.)* Chortle! Chortle! What! *(To Wilf.)* Besides I need someone with... *(Puts her arm in his again)* strong arms... like you. *(He makes an embarassed little whine)* End Jack's a bit of a pussy really. *(Pronounce it 'rarely'.)*
JACK	*(Enters cheerfully with a mimed cricket bat over his shoulder.)* I say cheps. Jus' saw your pater in his Sunday kit, Wilf. Got a match has he?
WILF	*(Pulls his arm out quickly.)* Ah! Jack!
BRIONY	Fellah's playing hard to get, my beloved.
JACK	What! Come on Wilf, ol' fellah. Play the game rather. Didn't expect *you* t' deliver a googly. Big match tomorrow. Versus

	Eastbourne in the County Cup.
BRIONY	*(Irritated.)* I say, Jack! I was talking about the play nort your cricket match.
WILF	Wha'?
JACK	Oh, I see. Need him to keep an end up, y'see. Whizzes 'em down like torpedoes. Harold Larwood incarnate, what.
BRIONY	Shut up, Jack.
JACK	*(Glum.)* Sorry!
BRONY	*(Takes Wilf's arm again. Flirtatious.)* Now Wilf. Chum!
JACK	I say! Steady on, Briony ol' thing! *(Sulks.)*
BRIONY	Disaster maximus if you won't do it!
WILF	Well, I…
BRIONY	Marvellous!
JACK	You can be a stinker sometimes, Briony! *(Storms off.)*
GERTIE	*(Enters. Beaming, then frowns as she sees Jack storming out.)* Topping day, you cheps! Topping day, rather. Topping day… Jack! Orf to a match are you? *(Flat disappointed.)* Joy in abundance rather.
BRIONY	I say! Wilf's just agreed to do it, Gertie dearest!
WILF	What! Bu'…
BRIONY	*(Launches into Macduff.)* Let us rather Hold fast the mortal sword, and like good men Bestride our down-fall'n birthdom:

	each new morn
	New widows howl, new orphans cry, new sorrows
	Strike heaven on the face, that it resounds
	As if it felt with Scotland and yell'd out
	Like syllable of dolour!
WILF	Now wait a minute! You don' wan' me to say all that, do yuh?
BRIONY	Of course, dear heart!
GERTIE	Oh, giggles in abundance!
WILF	Jack! *(Runs out after Jack.)*
GERTIE	*(Takes Briony's arm.)* I say, is Jack alright. Seemed miffed rather.
BRIONY	I took Wilf's arm so he sulked. *(Gertie shrieks.)*
GERTIE	You're such a flirt, Briony!
BRIONY	I know! Hoots in abundance! I just love the smell of his overalls. *(Dreamy.)* Motorcar tyres end axle grease. *(They both shriek.)* End isn't it a lovely day! As hot as hot end the Darns bright'n'green end smelling of hay. End the birds chettering end the crickets churring. End the cheps all big'n'hot in their overalls end cricket shirts. *(They both shriek again. She sighs.)* You wouldn't think there was a war on. I do so hope they don't all have to go away like the first one.

Music 4 – begins ('Til war came').

GERTIE   I hope not! Misery in abundance! Got to go chum. Helping Pa in the surgery today. Did you know his Austin Seven's gorn end bust its big end. Ta-ta! *(Exits.)*

BRIONY   *(Sings.)* The way we were is
The way we were.
It was all that we could know
'Til war came and swept things away
And the fields were left unmown.
And the way we are is
The way we are
And only time will show
Whether cricketers will always play on the green
And the WI meet in the hall
And the morris men dance at Christmas time
And the last couple go to the ball.
And the swallows will fly
And the magpies cry
'Til the last December goes
And the larks will sing above flint strewn fields
Over young men laid out in rows.
(Speaks.) Golly! Horrors maximus! I do hope it don't happen again.

Music 4 – ends

CANO 4

Swan Lake – *Simultaneously the edge of a lake and the birds' equivalent of an 'office', papers, pens, drawers, rubber stamps, etc*
Feather (M1), Cygnus (M2), Macbyrd (M3), Quill (M4), Pen (F1), Wormwood, Rosebud & Jenny Wren (F2)

Macbyrd flies in followed attentively by Wormwood. He is evasive, all the time reading & signing papers.

WORMWOOD	They said, 'The day of the swan is finally done?' But what does it…?
MACBYRD	They talked in riddles! Mischief, tha's all.
WORMWOOD	And that your day 'ad come?
MACBYRD	Yes. He said that the 'stream's frantic race froo the vale is run.'
WORMWOOD	What? Wha' on earth do tha' mean?
MACBYRD	And that 'Brook will be hay' an' fields become clay'.
WORMWOOD	'Brook will be 'ay and fields clay'?
MACBYRD	And that *(Stops signing & glares at the audience. Slowly.)* 'Oomans will march all over the green an' feet will run where lake 'as been!'
WORMWOOD	*(Forces him to look at her.)* But what does it mean?
MACBYRD	Riddles! That's all. Mischief! Magpies' gypsy mischief! *(Carries on signing.)*
WORMWOOD	*(Whispers clandestinely.)* An' tha' your time 'as come, Macbyrd!

MACBYRD	Quiet! *(Looks around in case someone is listening.)*
WORMWOOD	*(Hard. Demanding his attention.)* You're a dark winged bird. Your wings are sleek an' shiny an' black against the sky! It's time for you to rule; that's wha' they are saying. Over meadow an' rye! Oh, yes. Couldn't be clearer!
MACBYRD	*(Nervous. Checking about.)* Quiet, Wormwood! If you are 'eard….!
WORMWOOD	Can't yuh see? You're be'er than 'im. You care about the birds. You do wha's best. All 'e cares abou' – 'im an' tha' wife of 'is – is poncin' abou' an' preenin' an' glidin' with their 'eads 'eld arrogant an' 'aughty an' 'igh!
MACBYRD	*(Pause. Look at her.)* They're swans!
WORMWOOD	Jus' 'cause they got money!
MACBYRD	Royal birds.
WORMWOOD	An' 'cause they've always ruled!
MACBYRD	*(Thoughtful)* White an'… splendid an'… powerful. *(Glares at the audience again.)* Not even 'oomans can touch 'em.
WORMWOOD	Bu' you'll rip the legs off a frog! Won't yuh? When you want to. An' you've 'ad a sparrar or two before today.
MACBYRD	I 'ave not!
WORMWOOD	You know wha' they meant by a 'raven's kiss'!
MACBYRD	*(Turns on her. Whispers.)* Bu' a swan! Kark!

QUILL	*(Off.)* Macbyrd. Mayor!
MACBYRD	Quiet!
WORMWOOD	We will talk again. *(Flies out.)*

The double act of the camply cheerful Quill & Feather conduct the absurd everyday business of the Mayor of Aviana, signing papers, rubber stamping, tossing the papers to the air, etc.

QUILL	*(Flies in with Feather. They pause. Obsequious.)* Macbyrd. Mayor. May we?
MACBYRD	Come in.
QUILL	Papers! More papers!
FEATHER	And more! *(Macbyrd sighs.)*
QUILL	A mayor's work… *(Offers him a quill. He waves it away and uses his own.)*
FEATHER	Responsibilities!
MACBYRD	But what are these papers?
QUILL	*(Cheerful.)* Nothin'! *(Macbyrd signs the papers, then throws them into the air so that they have to fly to catch them.)*
FEATHER	Jus'… papers!
MACBYRD	But…
QUILL	A mayor's work…
FEATHER	Is never done. *(Offers him more papers.)*
MACBYRD	Oh! *(His pen gives up. He throws it away. Quill gives him another one plucked from his own body.)* Thank you, Quill.
QUILL	*(Reads from a list.)* The Daily Chirrup has published some gossip.

FEATHER	*(To the audience.)* Been watching 'er royalness through the reeds.
QUILL	Through the reeds! *(Gives him the relevant paper. He signs it & throws it away, etc.)*
FEATHER	*(Reads from a list.)* The magpies have been stealing eggs and building nests where they shouldn't. *(Gives him the paper, signs, etc, and so on.)*
QUILL	*(To the audience.)* Give them an inch and they'll…
FEATHER	*(Shakes his head in dismay.)* The coots are complaining.
QUILL	*(Reads.)* The wagtails can't pay their rent.
FEATHER	So we chucked 'em out.
MACBYRD	What! *(Takes the paper and goes to read it. Quill cautiously takes the paper back, smiling in a placatory way, indicates for Macbyrd to sign. He does then Quill throws it away. Macbyrd watches it in dismay.)*
QUILL	Then there's this. *(Points to the paper in Feather's hand.)*
FEATHER	*(Reads.)* 'Oomans… have been interfering with the swans' nest. *(Feather & Quill glare at the audience.)*
QUILL	*(Slowly. Threatening.)* Lake renovation work. *(Macbyrd signs and gives it to Quill who folds it up carefully & puts it in his pocket glaring at the audience.)*

FEATHER	*(Reads.)* And planning permission is required for swallows' dwellings in the barn.
QUILL	*(To the audience.)* Two up. Two down.
MACBYRD	Righ'. *(Takes the paper, signs it, stamps it, then throws it away, etc.)*
CYGNUS	*(Off.)* My dear!
QUILL	Look out! *(There's immediate panic.)*

Music 5 – The Swan dance begins.

FEATHER	They're here! *(Quill & Feather, and Macbyrd, a little more reluctantly, bow.)*

The swans trot awkwardly in, followed by Rosebud Coot who is trying to take a photo of them. They step into the lake – Vsfx – and elegantly glide around the water.

PEN	*(Proud.)* What a tiring morning, my dear.
CYGNUS	*(Arrogant.)* So much attention! *(To the audience.)* And why not?
QUILL/ FEATHER	*(Bowing.)* Your royalness!

As he swims Cygnus releases them from the bow, then indicates for them to bow again, releases them again, indicates for them to bow again, and so on, like a conductor controlling the rise and fall of an orchestra.

ROSEBUD	*(Gobsmacked. Utterly obsequious. To the audience.)* Oh, it's the best day of my life! To have seen them! *(To them.)* Would you? *(Tries to take a photo. They ignore her. Swimming close to them.)* I've read all about you in the Daily Chirrup!
CYGNUS	Have you? I'm not surprised.
ROSEBUD	I've always admired you.
CYGNUS	*(Discrete.)* Get rid of her, Quill. *(Quill & Feather spring into action.)*
QUILL	*(Guiding Rosebud away.)* This way please.
ROSEBUD	But I was just…
FEATHER	Admiring them, we know. *(They shoo her out.)*
PEN	So many 'oomans. Down by the lake.
CYGNUS	*(Sour.)* Especially the snotty nosed little ones.
PEN	Come to feed us with their…
CYGNUS	*(Glares at the audience.)* Stale bread…
FEATHER	*(Cheerful.)* And scones. *(Rhyme with 'cones'.)*
CYGNUS	*(Glares at him.)* Scones! *(To rhyme with 'cons'. Feather bows in obeisance. Sour.)* Ragamuffins sailing their miniature sailing boats with cotton rigging.
PEN	How they loved us! The 'oomans.
CYGNUS	Well, why wouldn't they?
PEN	How… white… we looked!
CYGNUS	Gliding elegantly.

PEN	Water droplets nestled on our fine sculptured backs…
CYGNUS	Grandmothers being indulgent.
PEN	Gleaming in the morning light!
CYGNUS	Grandpapas being… silly. Making absurd jokes. To impress the grandchildren! *(Sour. Imitates.)* Let's go to the pond and feed the ducks! *(Contempt.)* Ducks! I mean!
PEN	*(Looking at the water)* Look! *(Points at her reflection.)* Our reflection!
CYGNUS	*(Overcome.)* Oh! How beautiful I look, my darling Pen!
PEN	And I, my precious!
CYGNUS	*(Staring into the water.)* Were water lillies ever whiter?
PEN	Reeds more erect than our lovely necks?
CYGNUS	Did larks sound sweeter than our gentle churring and chuttering?
PEN & CYGNUS	We… are… so… lovely! *(Quill & Feather admire them. Macbyrd stays neutral. They churr with self-satisfaction, fluttering their eyelids at the audience.)*

Music 5 – ends.

QUILL	Your royalness, Jennifer… er… *(Checks his papers)* Wren is waitin' on the bank. Wishes to see you. *(Shaking his head.)* For some reason. *(Feather exits to get her.)*

CYGNUS	What? *(Contemptuous.)* Jennifer who…? *(Shakes his head not understanding.)*

She is brought in by Feather. She is small, shy and overwhelmed, an object on display.

MACBYRD	*(Takes the paper from Quill.)* The Wrens, Jenny, an' *(Checks a paper)*… er… Jack 'ave a small nest in the 'edgerow, your… royalness. *(Gives Cygnus the paper who studies it.)*
JENNIFER	*(Contorted with shame.)* Straw, my lord. That's all.
PEN	*(Contemptuous.)* Oh, the Hedgerow. That's one of those… estates isn't it? *(Looks at Jennifer.)* Oh dear.
MACBYRD	They need something bigger, but can' afford the rent.
CYGNUS	*(Unsympathetic.)* Do they?
MACBYRD	She's 'ad more babies recently, yuh see.
CYGNUS	*(Speaks loudly to her as if she's deaf.)* Oh. Been breeding, have you? *(She nods pathetically.)*
PEN	I expect it's the hot weather.
QUILL	Makes them more active.
CYGNUS	*(Speaks loudly again.)* More active, ay? *(She nods again.)*
FEATHER	The wrens are always at it, your royalness.
QUILL	Proper little gymnasts.
CYGNUS	*(Loudly.)* Little gymnasts, I hear? *(She

	nods again.)
PEN	Disgusting!
CYGNUS	Well, out of the question! *(Tosses the paper aside. To Jennifer.)* Breedless! That's the answer. Take it from me, young lady. Breed… less! Out you go. *(Quill hurries her out.)* Come on, my dear! *(Glides off with Pen around the lake.)*

Music 6 – The Swan dance reprise begins.

MACBYRD	Bu' Cygnus! Your royal…ness!
CYGNUS	All for the best, Macbyrd! All for the best! Don't worry so much. Enjoy the dance! The light on the lake! The heat on your back! The music! The glide!
PEN	I'll stay a while, husband, if you don't mind.

Cygnus bows to her, then flies out as she glides around the lake.

> All for the best! All for the best! Enjoy the dance! The light on the lake! The heat on your back! The music! The glide! How lovely it all is! How lovely… life… is!

Feather watches her, sighing with admiration, until finally she glides out with him following.

Music 6 – ends.

MACBYRD *(Angry.)* Breed less! Breed less! Wha' cold an' wivverin' 'earts are these tha' rule in Aviana? 'As a winter snow ever shrunk the life out of a delicate flower; a snowdrop or a daffodil sprung too early from an 'ard and stony earf? *(Hard.)* Is this my duty? Is this 'oo I serve? *(Exits bitterly.)*

CANO 5

NEWS – *Hillside cottage*
Wilf (M1), George & Hugo (M2), Jack (M3), Briony (F1) & Lil & Gertie (F2)

George enters on his Enfield. Lil comes out of the cottage as he turns the bike off, dismounts and pulls it up onto its stand.

LIL	I see yuh back then.
GEORGE	I am.
LIL	I 'eard yuh comin' up the road. *(He nods & takes his gauntlets off. Says nothing. Pause.)* Well? Cat go' yuh tongue then?
GEORGE	Yuh wunt believe it, Lil!
LIL	I wunt believe it? Come on! Tell me an' I'll sees if I wunt believe it.
GEORGE	(Slowly.) Mr Churchill wants Swan Meadow.
LIL	*(Shocked.)* Mr Churchill wants Swan Meadow! What does 'e wan' Swan Meadow for? Does he need an allotment?
GEORGE	No. I goes in this building, The War Office, on 'Orseguards Avenue. I found it alrigh'. An' there's this big staircase with brass banisters an' dark corridors and 'undreds of rooms like I dunno wha' – an' I knocks on room number 736 like it says in the letter an' *(Speaks posh for a moment),* 'Come in,' 'e says.

	It was that la-di-da Cedric Lilywhite! An' 'e's sitting on a big leather chair be'ind this huge desk with 'is little round specs an' 'is striped suit – an' 'e says, 'Cuppa tea, Mr Beeskep', so I 'as a cuppa tea, an' then 'e says... 'E would like to inform me that Mr Churchill 'as commandeered Swan Meadow to be... an airfield...for the RAF...for their Spitfires!
LIL	Spitfires! In Jevington? *(She gazes at the audience as if for support.)*
GEORGE	Tha's right. It's goin' arf any day!
LIL	Bu' wha' about the WI fete? Dora Pentlow in't gonna be 'appy! An' Briony's open air play – an' the cricket? They wunt be able to play. Jack Bannister in't gonna be best pleased is 'e! An' your vehicles be'ind the garage. You'll 'ave nowhere t'put 'em!
GEORGE	Tha's right. An' dad 'ad it afore me an' granddad an' 'is dad. It's always bin in the family an' used by the village. An' now they're goin' t'take it.
LIL	Bu' can they do tha'?
GEORGE	They can. They're goin' t'roll a strip of grass for a runway – an' they're goin' t'... *(Slowly)* fill in the brook an' the lake!
LIL	Fill in the brook an' the lake? Bu' wha' about the swans? Where they gonna go?

GEORGE	Mr Lilywhite says they can't risk any accidents with swans takin' arf jus' as a plane's comin' in or goin' arf. So they're goin' t' take 'em somewheres else.
LIL	Well, tha's a shock!
GEORGE	'E says that scrawny little Adolf is planning to invade!
LIL	Wha'!
GEORGE	An' the boys are gonna be called up, too. *(Quickly.)* Bu' yuh munt tell no-one, under the Treachery Act!
LIL	Oh! Not again!
GEORGE	They're goin' t'send a notice for you t'put up in the post office. In the meantime we munt say nothin'.
LIL	Bu' 'oo's gonna tell the birds, ay? They're goin' t'be whistlin' away in the sunshine, 'appy an' cheerful an' then all of a sudden *(Cross)* all these ruddy planes are gonna be roarin' past!
GEORGE	Don' say tha', Lil. Nothin's gonna be the same now. You see, it's for England an' the king. *(They unconsciously straighten their backs and look out over the meadow.)*
WILF	*(Enters.)* Well, I sees yuh back then.
LIL	Yes, 'e is. *(Goes indoors. George fiddles with his Enfield.)*
WILF	Well, I only axed. *(Pause.)* Yuh bin up t' London then?
GEORGE	Tha's right.

WILF	*(Pause.)* An' now yuh back.
GEORGE	Yes, I am.
WILF	Righ'. *(Pause.)* Wha' was it like then?
GEORGE	Busy.
WILF	Busy, ay?
GEORGE	Tha's wha' I said.
WILF	Righ'. *(Pause.)* Do anythin'… interestin'?
GEORGE	Yes.
WILF	Oh, righ'. Tha's good then. *(Pause.)* Did you 'ave a good time?
GEORGE	Fair t' middlin'.
WILF	Fair t' middlin'? Oh! *(Pause.)* Not gonna tell me what's goin' arf then?
GEORGE	No I in't. 'Sides they in't nothin' goin' aft, 'cept you down to the garage t'fix Dr Gordon's big end. *(Exits.)*
WILF	*(Calls after him.)* Well, I only axed! *(To the audience.)* Wha's eatin' them? I was only gonna tell Pop the big end 'ad arrived!
BRIONY	*(Enters arm in arm with Jack & with Gertie trailing behind. Calls out. Flirtatious.)* Coooie, Wilf! It's us!
WILF	Oh, no! It's Briony! *(Hurrying out.)* Sorry, Briony! Busy with Gertie's da's big end. *(Exits.)*
JACK	*(Put out.)* I say, Briony! There you go again! Cooing at Wilf!
BRIONY	Cooing? I didn't think I was cooing. Was I cooing, Gertie dearest?

GERTIE	Well you were cooing a little bit, Briony.
BRIONY	Well, unfairness in abundance! Kent a gell coo if she wants to?
JACK	*(Sulks.)* But you're aways cooing at some chep or other!
BRIONY	*(Takes his arm.)* Oh, my big grumpy badger!
GERTIE	Don't mind me!
BRIONY	A gell is only cooing after all. It's not like… kissing. *(A brief pause then she & Gertie shriek with laughter.)*

Music 7 – begins. 'The Flirt.'

JACK	But… *(Sings.)* On Monday there was Trevor down the bank! Then on Tuesday at the club you winked at Frank! Then on Wednesday at the ballet – D'you remember, you and Sally? - You pinched ol' Woofy's bottom for a prank! Then on Thursday when we visited the zoo, With Milly and her dreadful cousin Sue, You chatted all the day In the most outrageous way With Milly's elder brother! *(To Gertie.)* Who was it?

GERTIE	Hugh.
JACK	It's just not fair when summer's in the air
And lovers walk across the Darns without a care
That you and I are not entwined
With a spaniel just behind
While brarn *(sic)* eyed cows fondly stand and stare.

But then on Friday at the club you sat with John.
Daisy mentioned you were practically gone!
And once you'd done the teas
Of cucumber and cheese
You were orf out in the nets with Charles and Ron!

And on Saturday – Well, I didn't want to bicker –
But with Rex you were – Damn it! – even quicker,
Running through the trees (you were),
At times almost on your knees –
And then on Sunday you went and whistled at the vicar! |

Music 7 – ends

BRIONY	*(Takes his arm affectionately.)* Oh, you

	silly chump!
GERTIE	Don't mind me!
BRIONY	*(Flirtatious.)* Don't be so jealous, dearest. Surely you know I'm not in love with Trevor. Hideous maximus! He has eyebrows like a privet hedge end I could never be in love with a privet hedge. End it's not my fault that Frank is such a flirt. End Woofy's bottom *was* sticking out in a rather cute sort of way. I couldn't resist, you see. End Huw is so good about zoos end I do *love* zoos. End John. Well… John is handsome! I have to admit. *(Dreamy for a moment).* But ebsolutely no good at all under a full moon. End I wasn't rarely running through the trees with Rex. There was a wasp, you see, end you know how tirribly frightened I am of wasps. And the vicar! The vicar! *(Hoots.)* He… is… such a hoot! And…

A sports car comes roaring in & skids to a halt.

HUGO	*(Jumps out.)* I say! Ken anyone point me to… *(Checks a piece of paper)* Swan Meadow?
BRIONY	*(Hypnotised.)* Swan Meadow?
HUGO	*(Kisses her hand.)* Well hello! Charmed!
BRIONY	*(All smiles.)* I'll take you there if you like.

JACK	I say!
HUGO	*(All eyes for her.)* Will you? Will you really? *(Rhyme with rarely.)*
BRIONY	*(Dazzled.)* I'd love to.
JACK	*(Hurt.)* Briony!
HUGO	Jolly good of you, ol' gell! Jump in *(He helps her in.)*
JACK	*(Cross.)* Briony!
BRIONY	Thet way! *(Points. As they roar off.)* Won't be long, chums!
JACK	*(Panicky)* Briony! *(Runs off after her at speed.)*
GERTIE	*(To the audience.)* Golly! Who was thet? *(Runs off more slowly after them.)*

CANO 6

MACBYRD PLEADS FOR THE SPARROWS – *The same*
Feather & Peter (M1), Cygnus (M2), Macbyrd (M3), Quill (M4), Pen (F1), & Pegotty (F2)

QUILL	*(Quill enters with papers & pen with Feather following.)* Item 4C, sub-section 3, the vicinity of the lake, antisocial behaviour thereto. *(Pause.)* The crows?
FEATHER	Hopping! Constantly hopping! Large numbers of them, congregating around the lake, and… hopping! And what's more, leaving their… deposits.
QUILL	I see. T-t-t-t-t! *(Writes.)* Recommendations to the mayor. That the crows… *(Slowly)* hop less in the vicinity of the lake. With particular attention to… the… leaving… of deposits. *(Pause.)* Moorhens?
FEATHER	Strutting! Strutting about – and bobbing their heads in a perculiar pecking motion. Constantly. *(Demonstrates.)*
QUILL	*(Looks at him.)* But they're moorhens. That's what moorhens do.
FEATHER	Yes, but they should leave it to the professionals. *(Shows the professional way to do it.)*
QUILL	*(Scowls at him.)* Yerrs. *(Forcefully striking the item out in his papers.)* Sparrows?
FEATHER	*(Stern.)* They want to build another nest! In the willows!

QUILL	What! Sparrows? In the willows! Absolutely not! Oh! No, no, no, no, no. The swans aren't going to like that. Not one bit! Sparrows in the willows?
FEATHER	*(Looking off.)* Look out! They're coming!

Cygnus sweeps in with Pen & Macbyrd behind.

CYGNUS	*(Contempt.)* But sparrows, Macbyrd!
MACBYRD	Yes, but…
CYGNUS	You say they want to speak to me? First wrens and now… sparrows!
QUILL	*(To Macbyrd.)* He's right.
FEATHER	*(Contempt.)* So… brown.
QUILL	And small.
FEATHER	So plain. Not like a heron with our long elegant… *(Smart arsed striding about until he's put down with a glare from Cygnus.)*
PEN	*(To Macbyrd.)* Two a penny!
MACBYRD	*(Pleads.)* But they're 'ere, your… royalness. Couldn't you jus'… speak to them?
CYGNUS	Well… if we must. Let them in then. *(Indicates to Feather to go & get them. He exits.)*
MACBYRD	*(Bows.)* Thank you, your… royalness.
PEN	Pointless! Why bother? The hedgerows used to be so lovely!
CYGNUS	In the old days.

PEN	The blackthorn and may!
CYGNUS	The hazel and field maple!
PEN	Honeysuckle and blackberries! Dizzy with old man's beard!
CYGNUS	A traveller's joy!
PEN	The dormice tucked up in their little nests. They didn't breed too much!
QUILL	*(Emphatic.)* Oh, *they* bred less! Much less.
PEN	Until the sparrows started filling the hedgerows.
QUILL	Worse than the wrens!
PEN	Always at it!
QUILL	Like rats.
PEN	Flies. Clouds of them. Eating all the berries! *(She starts gliding round the lake.)* Pointless seeing them! We need to sift out the weak – like a spider's web.
QUILL	Like a pond. *(Pleased with himself.)*
PEN	Exactly! The fish hatch the eggs, the eggs become larvae, the flies eat the larvae, the fry eat the flies, the fish eat the fry…
QUILL	And the swans eat the fish. *(Pen & Cygnus glare at him.)* Just little ones, of course.
CYGNUS	Shut up, Quill! *(Quill immediately goes into a servile position.)*
PEN	*(Warming to it.)* But the lake is so lovely with everything in its place.

	The boatmen paddling their little legs on the surface, the frogs plopping from stone to stone, the shadowy pike gliding menacingly along the bottom and the bream and carp basking in the sparkling sunlight under the willows.
PETER	*(Peter & Pegotty fly in sheepishly. A very small voice.)* Excuse me, but…
CYGNUS	*(Sees them.)* Ah! *(Over friendly.)* Come in! Come in! Peter isn't it? *(Peter nods.)* And… *(Starts checking through his papers.)*
MACBYRD	Pegotty.
CYGNUS	*(With enthusiasm.)* Pegotty! Welcome! Welcome! It's always good to have a visit from the… er…
QUILL	*(Leans over & whispers.)* Riff raff.
CYGNUS	*(Glares at him.)* Er…
QUILL	Hoi polloi?
CYGNUS	*(Glares again.)* Er… populace. Always good to see the populace. In fact I saw one only the other day.
PETER & PEG	*(Very small voices.)* Thank you, your royalness.
CYGNUS	Now, what can I do for you? I understand you are having trouble with your… er… *(Checks his papers)* nest? Too small or something?
PEGOTTY	Just twigs, sir. A bundle of twigs.
PETER	And we 'ave a lot of….
CYGNUS	Babies? Yerrs. I thought so.

	(Benevolent.) How nice. *(Patient.)* Well, tell me what do you want me to do about it?
PETER	We'd like to build another nest, sir…
PEGOTTY	In the willows.
PEN	*(General uproar. Yells.)* The willows! *(All'improvviso. 'The willows! They want to build a nest in the willows. Ridiculous! Etc.')* You mean by the lake? Just over there? Where the branches hang languidly in the summer heat and the sun sparkles on the water while mayfly larvae and other prey glide temptingly by? Conveniently situated near amenities and local services?
PETER	*(A very small voice.)* Yes.
CYGNUS	Out of the question!
MACBYRD	But they would nest 'igh, my lord. They wouldn't be a problem. *(To Pen.)* Each as you say in their own place. They wouldn't eat the larvae, or the fish, ma'am. They don't eat pond food. Sparrars don't. They would just be a few sparrars among the many 'undreds of birds – in their own nest and content with their lot.
CYGNUS	*(Fierce.)* But *not* in the willows, Macbyrd. The lake is for swans…
QUILL	*(Just audible.)* And geese.
CYGNUS	And the hedgerow is for sparrows!
PEN	And goodness knows what the coots would say!

QUILL	And the moorhens.
CYGNUS	I've made my decision.
QUILL	And the ducks and…
CYGNUS	*(Turns on him.)* Shut your beak, Quill! *(Quill shrinks into subservience.)*
MACBYRD	But, Cygnus… My lord. What are they to do? They have too many babies for their…
CYGNUS	Yerrs. *(Slowly.)* More little gymnasts no doubt. *(To Peter and Pegotty.)* Take my advice, Peter and Pegotty. Breed… less!
MACBYRD	Bu'…
CYGNUS	*(Turns on him.)* Macbyrd! On which side of the lake do you nest?
MACBYRD	*(Pause.)* Yours, your… *(Bows, but half-heartedly.)*
CYGNUS	*(Glares at him.)* I hope so. *(Raises his wings to make him look very big, then exits with Pen & Quill in tow.)*
PEGOTTY	Oh dear! Oh dear, oh dear! *(Flies out distressed.)*
PETER	*(After a moment of silence.)* Thank you, sir. We are… very much obliged. Very much… obliged indeed, sir. *(Drops his head.)* I… I… wanted you… to know. *(Pause for a while as Macbyrd sighs & shakes his head, then waves him away as if to say: Don't worry.)* Fank you, sir. *(Flies out.)*
MACBYRD	*(Slowly.)* 'Oo is this bird tha' struts an' glides an' wears 'is smiles like a mask?

(Pause.) Does 'is 'eart beat like a bird? *(Pause.)* Is 'is flesh warm like a bird... *(Pause)* like a dead sparrow just caught by a cat tha' lies soft an' still in the 'and of a boy? *(Pause.)* No! 'E's cold like a fish. 'E should prowl the shadowy bottom with 'is fierce whiskers an' snap at the fry an' rip the breast from a warty toad! *(Sighs.)* Let me breathe the 'igh summer air, not 'is foul dank water. *(Flies off.)*

CANO 7

ANOTHER STRANGER ARRIVES AS THE GIRLS BICKER – *The same*

Briony (F1), Gertie (F2), Cedric Lilywhite (M3) & Professor Bhattacharjeee (M4)

BRIONY	*(Enters with Gertie who seems annoyed.)* Manliness maximus, Gertie! *(Lovingly.)* Wing Commander Hugo Ffinch-Hatton! *(Sighs.)*
GERTIE	*(Miffed but polite.)* If you say so.
BRIONY	*(Links arms.)* He leapt out of the car like Errol Flynn in The Dawn Patrol, swung round to the passenger side, put his hend round my back end swept me out in one fell swoop! Very particular he was in his menners – end such a firm grip.
GERTIE	*(Indifferent.)* Oh.
BRIONY	I especially liked his hends. Rather long end soft like a doctor's hends but brarn *(sic)* and strong.
GERTIE	Really.
BRIONY	But mystery in abundance, Gertie! Didn't say a thing. Just took one look at the meadow, said how charming the lake was, shook my hend end then went to The Eight Bells. End, the lake was so pretty! End it's such a lovely day! With the birds twittering cheerfully end the fish popping up with their little mouths to snaffle up the insects. Then plopping right down again!

GERTIE	*(Irritable.)* Yes, I suppose so.
BRIONY	You suppose so? *(Irritated herself now.)* It's Miss Supposed-so, is it? Well you couldn't have a much nicer summer day than this! Cheerfulness in abundance if you ask me!
GERTIE	*(Cross.)* It might be for you, Miss Hoi-ti-toi, but I wouldn't say it was for Jack.
BRIONY	Jack! What has he got to do with it?
GERTIE	Well, you are my very best friend, Briony, but it is important to tell the truth, especially to one's very best friends end… end… the truth is I think you were rather horrid to him this morning!
BRIONY	Horrid? Was I?
GERTIE	Cooing all over the wing commander.
BRIONY	Cooing? I wasn't cooing! Beastliness in abundance, Gertie! *(Pulls her arm out from Gertie's irritably.)* Besides, we aren't engaged so I don't see why I shouldn't coo when I want to!
GERTIE	So you *were* cooing! End if you hold a chep's hend end call him your grumpy little badger, then that's practically engaged!
BRIONY	Grumpy little badger! Do you know, I think you are in love with him yourself!
GERTIE	I am not! End you've no call to be catty! End I think I'll call it good day. *(Storms off in a sulk.)*

BRIONY	Gertie! Don't let's fight! *(Cedric Lilywhite enters studying a map.)* Oh, beastliness! *(Turns round & he's right in front of her.)* Oh!
CEDRIC	Ma'am. Would you? *(Points to the map.)* Could you… oblige? Em I in the vicini'y of… er… Hillside Co'age by any chance?
BRIONY	Oh. Yes. Not far. The Beeskeps.
CEDRIC	Indeed. Mr George Beeskep in partic'a'lar. La'itude *(Checks)* 50.794590. Longitude 0.21623661. If you would be so kind.
BRIONY	I don't know the latitude, but they live just over there. *(She points.)*

Music 8 – begins.

CEDRIC	*(Checks a compass.)* That's the Norf. That's the East. Let me see. Indeed they do, ma'am. I em much obliged. *(A lark begins to sing. He studies the sky.)* Ah! D'you 'ear thet? A lark. Pretty li'le thing. Mrs Lilywhite, my… er… wife… She particklilly likes the lark. She do often note 'ow 'igh they fly. Yes. Up there in the… light. Above everyfing. The turmoil an' troubles. She do say thet. Mrs Lilywhite. *(Begins to walk off.)*
BRIONY	Really? *(Calls after him.)* Oh! Excuse me! I think Mr Beeskep might be in

	the post office just there. *(Points.)* I saw him talking to Mrs Beeskep just now. She works there, you see.
CEDRIC	Thenk you! Thet's very kind. I'll try the post office. Much obliged, miss. *(Raises his hat.)*
BRIONY	*(Watches him go.)* Lor'! Who was thet? *(To the audience.)* Two strangers in the village on the same day! How curious! *(Looks after him again.)* Trotting orf like a stripy beetle, or… or… a clock on legs.

Professor Bhattacharjee, a lark, flies in. He flies in an Indian style aerial dance with a light & elegant carelessness, bathing in the light as a sparrow does in dust.

    Oh, look! The lark! And he is so very pretty, too! Singing his little head orf as if he hasn't got a care in the world! Maybe he hasn't. Pretty little thing. *(To the audience again.)* Criky! *(Remembering Gertie.)* Oh! Where's she gone? *(Runs off.)* Gertie! Wait for me!

CANO 8

THE LIGHT – *High above the Downs*
Macbyrd (M3), & Professor Bhattacharjeee (M4)

Music 8 – ends.

MACBYRD	*(Macbyrd enters after a while. Bhattacharjee hovers, head on one side, looking at him. Macbyrd is upset & angry.)* Let me breave! Let me breave! *(Panting.)* 'E's a fish! A fish! Cold like a fish. 'E should prowl the shadowy bottom with his fierce whiskers, 'e should! What does 'e know about sparrows! Snap at the fry, 'e should; rip at the breast of a warty toad! 'E ain't no bird – wiv 'is 'ead 'eld 'igh! Poncin' an' preenin'! Poncin' an' preenin'! Oh! Let me breave.
BHATTA	*(Very polite & cheerful.)* Fish? *(Smiles broadly.)*
MACBYRD	Wha'?
BHATTA	You won't find fish up here. Not up in the light. Not in the usual run of things. No, no, no, no, no. Spiders. Lots of spiders. You'd be surprised. Most surprising. *(Wagging his head thoughtfully.)*
MACBYRD	I wasn't…
BHATTA	Grasshoppers, caterpillars, bugs. There are many and various kinds. But not

fish. Not as a rule. Caught by the wind they are. One minute gobbling away at a leaf or making their little silvery webs, then... Woosh! Up they come, carried by the wind up into the wide open space of air and light... released, as I like to say, from all Earth's troubles and tribulations.

MACBYRD But you do eat 'em presumably?

BHATTA Oh, yes. Ladybirds, moths... *(Snatches one and eats it)* butterflies.

MACBYRD *(Less than interested.)* Yeh... Interestin'.

BHATTA You are most welcome. *(Bows.)*

MACBYRD An' 'oo may you be then? I ain't come across you before in Aviana. Not in these parts. We don't get many foreigners. Not in Jevington.

BHATTA Professor Bhattacharjee *(Bows, hands together)* of the Saraswati School for Indian bushlarks, Calcutta.

MACBYRD Calcu'a!

BHATTA Mirafra erythroptera to be precise. We are distinguished from Jerdon's bush lark – Mirafra affinis – by our longer tail, shorter bill and legs. The twitchers are most excited if I may say so, jumping about with their binoculars and Kodak Brownie 127's! Most amusing!

MACBYRD But how...?

BHATTA I know! It is indeed quite splendidly surprising and amusing, but caught up

	I was in a tropical storm over the Bay of Bengal and carried by the wind high in the atmosphere to this very place. *(Shaking his head & smiling profusely.)* It is indeed remarkable! And *(Bows again)* may I presume to ask your name?
MACBYRD	Macbyrd. Raven. *(Pause. Bitter.)* Mayor of these parts.
BHATTA	I am honoured. Mayor indeed, Mr Macbyrd. A bird of some position. *(Bows again, hands together.)* Nevertheless, I note for example your concern for the humble sparrow who, as I am sure you know, bathes his chubby little body in the dust while you and I so luckily bathe in the crystal pure air of heaven.
MACBYRD	What?

Music 9 – begins.

BHATTA	It has indeed been a great pleasure. *(Looking up.)* But the sun is high and most welcoming, so I must… *(Hypnotised by the light as he gazes into the sky. Flies off.)*
MACBYRD	*(Flies after him)* But Professor Bhatta…! Whad'yuh say yuh name was? You'll let me fly wiv you if I may!
BHATTA	You are most welcome. But I fly high

	you know. Very high! High, high, high above all the bluster and bravado, the swagger and swish, as I like to say.
MACBYRD	But not too 'igh mind. I get a bit out of breath up 'ere. *(They fly out.)*

Music 9 – ends & Music 10 – begins.

CANO 9

THE WORD IS OUT – *Jevington Post Office*
Wilf (M1), George (M2), Jack & Cedric (M3), PC Alf Wood (M4), Dora Pentlow (F1) & Lil (F2)

As each character enters & leaves make the sound of the door as a vsfx.

LIL	*(Enters & begins sorting letters.)* What's this? *(Finds a large envelope.)* The War Office! *(Takes out a letter.)* This is it. I'd better put it up. *(She pins up the notice on the board.)* They in't gonna like this.
DORA	*(Comes storming in, followed by George and Wilf.)* Where is it?
WILF	What's goin' arf, ma?
LIL	Mrs Pentlow! *(Patient.)* Dora. It's over there, on the board. It come this mornin' from the War Office in a brown envelope marked 'Urgent' in red. It's a proper official notice mind. I've just put it up. Now did you want stamps? *(Busies herself.)*
DORA	*(Reads the notice. Sings.)* Filling in the pond! Digging up the green! It's outrageous! It's preposterous! It's obscene!
WILF	*(Speaks.)* Digging up the green? What the…!
GEORGE	*(Speaks.)* I've 'eard nothin'.

DORA	And what about the fête?
	And the flower show! *(Speaks)* When's the date, Lil? *(Studies the notice.)*
	Believe me, they couldn't care a bean!
LIL	*(Studies the notice. Speaks.)* The fifth.
DORA	The fifth!
WILF	But that's today!
DORA	They're starting work today!
	But we've hardly had a chance to have our say.
	(Speaks.) And I've got a lot to say about it, I tell you!
	(Sings.) The women will be furious! *And* Marge has baked the cakes for us!
	(Churchillian.) This is indeed a dark and dismal day!
PC ALF WOOD	*(Enters with Jack.)* Well I sees you're all gathered then.
DORA	We're all gathered alright, PC Wood, and want to know what's going on!
PC WOOD	*(Takes his notebook out.)* Now, I put down in my notebook, jus' what the Super said. Look!
	(Reads.) 'The fifth of June. A runway on the green.'
	(Uproar. All'improvviso: 'A runway! What for? For the RAF. Etc.)

	It's there in black an' white
	So there in't no need to fight !
	It's come from up above. That's all I've seen. *(Closes his notebook.)*
JACK	But what about the cricket! Max has mown the wicket
	And we've got a match Sunday, don-cha-know!
	You really ought to know.
	The cheps'll be upset! –
	We won't even get a net! –
	And we fixed it months and months ago.

Music 10 – ends.

DORA	*(Speaks.)* Why can't they put it in Polegate? That's what I want to know!
LIL	Well, I think it'll be nice 'avin' more young men in the village. I believe the RAF are t'be billeted at the Manor. In't tha' right, Alf?
JACK	I say! Jevington Manor! But that's… Briony's pad!
PC WOOD	*(Nodding fervently.)* Yes, that's right. You're quite right, Lil. Jevington Manor.
JACK	*(Upset. Storms out.)* But… but… but… but… There'll be all those cheps! I say! That's jolly bad form! Briony! Briony! Where is she? *(Exits.)*

LIL	*(Calls after him.)* Now! Don't be like tha', Jack. No need t'panic.

Music 11– begins.

> *(To the audience.)* You see the green in June is such a pretty thing
> When daisies bloom an' skylarks fly – an' sing
> Their little 'earts out 'overin'
> Above the mown grass bustlin'
> With cricketers an' dogs an' suchlike things.
> An' it's not a minor ma'er to 'ear a bureaucrat cha'er
> About change an' strange an' other curious things
> Tha' send the slow an' steady day
> Into a sway of bluster an' dismay
> An' calm hearts into a fearful flutter.

Music 11– ends.

WILF	*(Blustering.)* Bu' never mind all tha'! What about the garage? We gotta park the motors somewheres. They've always bin on the green. It in't right!
PC WOOD	Now then! Now then, young Wilf! I'taint no use gettin' in a stew. The Super rang me up this mornin' an' tol' me tha'…

DORA	It's alright you saying that, Alf Wood, but the WI won't stand for it, I'm telling you! *(Turns on George.)* And why are you, George Beeskep, handing over your field without so much as a by your leave? I notice you haven't said much. Some supporter of the village you are! A… a… traitor, you are! *(All'improvviso: 'Wait a minute! Now 'ang on, Dora! Etc.')*
PC WOOD	Now then! Now then, Mrs Pentlow! Let's not 'ave any of tha'!
WILF	But' what's goin' arf? Wha' d'they wan' an airfield for? I'm only axin'!
LIL	Yuh Pop will tell yuh. Come on George.
GEORGE	Yuh can all get in a stew, but 'taint nothin' we can do about it. They've commandeered my field an' that's the truth.
WILF	'Oo 'as?
GEORGE	The War Ministry. For spitfires an' 'urricanes. *(Speaks to Dora.)* So it in't no use bein' stuck up and aloof.
PC WOOD	It's the law an' that's the end on it.
MR LILYWHITE	*(Enters. Hesitant. They all stare at him.)* Ah. Yes… Er… I would be much obliged if someone could tell me. Em I in the post office?
LIL	You are – an' wha' can I do for you, sir?
MR LILYWHITE	I was lookin' for Mr Bee…
GEORGE	*(Suddenly realises who it is.)* Oh! Mr

	Lilywhite. You're 'ere! In the... er... village.
MR LILYWHITE	Ah, Mr Beeskep. I wonder if you might oblige. I 'ev come to inspect your field.
DORA	*(On her high horse.)* And who might this be?
GEORGE	This is…
MR LILYWHITE	Mr Cedric Lilywhite. Secretary to the Under Secretary to the Minister of War and… Prime Minister, Mr Winston Churchill.
DORA	*(Knocked back.)* Oh, I see.
MR LILYWHITE	*(Stretching out his hand to her.)* And who might I be addressin', medam?
DORA	Dora Pentlow. WI. *(They shake hands limply. Brief pause as she regains her momentum, but posher now.)* End I suppose we hev you to thenk for this…
MR LILYWHITE	The WI? Mrs Lilywhite, my wife, is a member of the WI. An intrepid, doughty and adroit organisation, if I may say so, 'oo will be much needed in the dark days to come.
DORA	Oh. Er… yes, well…
MR LILYWHITE	Mrs Lilywhite do say thet.
DORA	Does she indeed? *(Slightly on the back foot.)* You see, Mr Lilypond, we were to have our fête and flower show on the green – *and* what about Briony's play!
MR LILYWHITE	Oh, I see. Mrs Lilywhite do love 'er flowers. Regularly exhibits, she does.

DORA   (*High horse again.*) I dare say Mrs Lilypond has many opinions on many matters, but what we want to know is what's to be done! (*Stabbing her finger on the counter.*)

WILF   (*Forceful.*) An' we'll 'ave no-where to put the cars at the garage! What's t'be done about tha' then?

GEORGE   Wilf! Tha's enough. (*To Mrs Lilywhite.*) 'E's my son. Don't take no notice of 'im.

MR LILYWHITE   Ah, Mr Wilf Beeskep. (*Shakes his hand firmly.*) I em afraid, sir, there won't *be* many cars about as such… (*General uproar.*) Petrol rationing, y'see. (*All'improvviso.*)

WILF   (*Shocked.*) But… wha' am I…?

MR LILYWHITE   (*Enthusiastic.*) A mechanic, Mr Beeskep? Thet is fortui'ous. The RAF will need mechanics. (*Makes a note in a notebook.*) For the planes, d'you understand? At the airfield. (*Writes in a notebook.*) Will Beeskep. Mechanic.

WILF   (*Not quite taking it in.*) Oh. Righ'.

MR LILYWHITE   (*Addressing them all. Slowly.*) You see, nothin' will be quite the same for a while. We will all hev to… er… adjust. (*Looking at Dora.*) The flowers, 'owever, beautiful, will become… vegetables, if you see what I mean. (*Looking at Wilf.*) Cars will become planes. (*Now them all.*) End the play will, so to speak,

	ascend from the field to the… er… sky. *(They all slowly look up.)*
DORA	Oh, well, yes… I suppose…
GEORGE	Oh, look at the time! Nearly eleven o'clock an' the prime minister is to speak on the BBC. 'Scuse us, Mr Lilywhite. Turn the wireless on Lil.

Music 12 – begins.

They gather round the wireless. Vsfx four pips.

ANNOUNCER	This is the BBC Home Service. We are interrupting the programme for an announcement by the Prime Minister, the Right Honourable Sir Winston Churchill.
CEDRIC	What General Weygand called The Battle of France is over… *(Closes his briefcase & leaves.)*
LIL	This is it! This is it! *(She turns the volume up.)*
WILF	The Battle of Britain is about… *(He shakes hands with George & exits.)*
ALF	…to begin.
LIL	Upon this battle depends the survival of Christian civilisation.
GEORGE	Upon it depends our own British life,
DORA	…and the long continuity of our institutions…
LIL	…and our Empire.

DORA	The whole fury and might of the enemy…
GEORGE	…must very soon be turned on us. *(George shakes Wilf's hand & Wilf leaves.)*
ALF	Hitler knows that he will have to break us in this island,
GEORGE	…or lose the war.
DORA	If we can stand up to him, all Europe may be freed…
LIL	and the life of the world may move forward into…
DORA	…broad, sunlit uplands.
ALF	But if we fail, then the whole world,
LIL	…including the United States,
DORA	…including all that we have known and cared for,
ALF	…will sink into the abyss of a new dark age.
DORA	Let us therefore brace ourselves to our duties… *(Determinely gathers her bags together & leaves.)*
GEORGE	…and so bear ourselves,
ALF	…that if the British Empire and its Commonwealth last for a thousand years… *(Pats George on the shoulder, then leaves.)*
LIL	…men will still say,
GEORGE	This was their finest hour. *(Lil switches off the wireless. They hug, then leave arm in arm. They stop, ponder for a moment at the magnitude of the events to come & then leave. Vsfx as the door closes.)*

CANO 10

A RAVEN'S KISS – *The brook flowing from the pond.*
Thorn (M1), Cygnus (M2), Macbyrd (M3) & Wormwood (M2)

Music 12 – ends.

MACBYRD	*(Flies in gasping for air. Followed by Thorn who watches him silently from a distance. Mutters. Seething.)* He ain't a bird! Kark! Wha' kind of bird is 'e? Poncin' an' preenin'! What does 'e know about sparrars! *(Bitter.)* An' 'is wife! The flies eat the larvae, the fry eat the flies, the fish eat the fry, an' the swans eat the fish! An' 'oo will eat the… *(Looks around in case someone is listening. Doesn't see Thorn. Pause)*? Cold! Cold! Like a warty toad! *(Shivers. Thorn perches nearby, but Macbyrd ignores him.)*
THORN	*(Pause.)* Bad day?
MACBYRD	What!
THORN	Cigarette?
MACBYRD	*(Pause, then Macbyrd takes one.)* Yeh. Go on then.
THORN	*(They sit side by side smoking for a moment.)* He's there you know. Just over there. *(Nods in the direction.)*
MACBYRD	What? *(Calmer, without force.)* Wha's yuh mischief, magpie? Off with you.

THORN	By the babbling brook. Among the reeds. *(Slight pause.)* Alone. *(Macbyrd wants to look at him, but doesn't.)* Long neck erect. His eyes yellow and black and hard like stones. His firm back dappled with water, jewels glistening in the sunlight, preening his strong white feathers. He's not on the lake. There are 'oomans by the lake. Digging. Things are… happening, Macbyrd. Things are… changing. *(Macbyrd turns sharply to him, studying him.)* *(Slowly.)* 'Oomans will march all over the green and feet will run where lake has been. Dark winged birds will rule meadow an' rye Sleek an' shiny an' black against sky!
MACBYRD	Enough! Kark! *(Chases him away. Thorn flies out as Wormwood flies in. She watches him go suspiciously.)*
WORMWOOD	Where've yuh bin? I've bin lookin' all over for yuh! They all 'ave! Fevver an' Quill! You've got papers t'sign! Papers! Lots of papers!
MACBYRD	Papers! I'm sick of papers!
WORMWOOD	Bu' yuh the mayor. Course yuh got papers. What's the ma'er wiv yuh? An' there are 'oomans by the lake wiv

	machines. Diggin' fings up! Somefin's 'appenin'!
MACBYRD	Wha' kind of machines?
WORMWOOD	Jus' machines! I've bin lookin' for yuh. Where've yuh bin?
MACBYRD	*(Looking up at the sky.)* Up there! Up there!
WORMWOOD	Up there? Wha' yuh doin' up there?
MACBYRD	I needed t' get closer t' the light. I needed t'breave.
WORMWOOD	*(Doesn't understand.)* What?
MACBYRD	There was a lark. A foreigner.
WORMWOOD	A lark? A foreigner? What d'yuh mean? We in't got no foreigners in Jevington. Not in all Aviana.
MACBYRD	'E was there I tell you! High up. Really high. Up in the light. Right up near the sun. It was like… bathin' in light!
WORMWOOD	What's the ma'er wiv yuh? *(Cygnus flies in.)* Yuh gotta… *(Sees Cygnus.)* Look out! It's Cygnus. *(Turns & right into Macbyrd's face. Slowly.)* An' 'e's alone! *(She flies out as Cygnus skids to a stop.)*

Music 13 – begins.

CYGNUS	Ah, Macbyrd just the chap I wanted to speak to. Now, these sparrows…
MACBYRD	Your royal-ness! *(Half bows. Going towards him.)* I am… loyal, you know. I…

CYGNUS	*(Uneasy.)* Yes. Of course. Of course. But… er… I…
MACBYRD	I went up into the light, yuh see.
CYGNUS	What?
MACBYRD	I wanted to make sure you… you… *(Going foward & laying his head in the crook of Cygnus' neck)* understood.
CYGNUS	*(Not sure how to respond.)* Yes, of course I understand.
MACBYRD	*(To the audience.)* And the swan lay down by the worried brook An' cried aloud to choughs an' rooks
CYGNUS	What does this mean? What's this? What's this?
MACBYRD	A raven's kiss. That's all. Just this. *(Kisses his neck.)*
CYGNUS	Ah! A kiss!
MACBYRD	*(To the audience.)* Said the swan.
CYGNUS	So you love me still. *(To the audience.)* An' the raven sighed.
MACBYRD	I do an' I will. An' they wrapped their necks like lovers will An' lay by the nest breaving 'ard until… *(He pecks Cygnus' neck hard.)*
CYGNUS	*(Shrieks in pain.)* Aaagghh!

Cygnus staggers to his feet & flapping violently tries to get into the air as he pulls a piece of long red frabric from his neck. Macbyrd holds him tenderly like a lover.

MACBYRD　　　The sun… painted red… the vale… an' the 'ill.

Trying to escape Cygnus dances a dance of 'the dying swan', comic, but shocking. Trying to escape, he winds the fabric round his body. They turn round and round slowly until Cygnus is able to pull away & flap out. Macbyrd slowly flies out in the opposite direction.

Music 13 – ends.

INTERVAL

CANO 11

THE DANCE – *The village hall.*
Wilf (M1), George & Hugo (M2), Jack (M3), Alf & Biffy (M4), Dora & Briony (F1) and Lil & Gertie (F2)

Music 14 – begins & ends.

LIL	*(Lil, George, PC Alf Wood and Mrs Dora Pentlow enter.)* But Dora…
MRS PENTLOW	No, I want it recorded in the minutes of the village hall committee that the decision was not unanimous. *I* did not vote for it!
ALF	Would you like me to inform Mr Churchill of tha' fac' personally, Mrs Pentlow? *(Laughter from George.)*
MRS PENTLOW	*(Scowls at him.)* And what's happening to the oak tree? Are they going to dig that up, too? That's what I want to know. *(To the audience.)* It was planted when Queen Victoria herself came to the throne. That's how old it is. *(To Lil.)* You can put that in the minutes as well!
GEORGE	I s'pose you was on the committee tha' organised it, ay Mrs Pentlow?
LIL	George!
PC WOOD	*(More laughter.)* You don' 'ave t'worry yuhself about no oak, Dora; it's stayin' righ' where it is. I can assure you.
LIL	Well, I think it will be nice 'avin' all these young men in the village,

	'specially as they're 'ere to defend King an' country. *(All'improvviso: "Ear, 'ear! I should think so, too. Etc.')*
PC WOOD	I'm be'ind you there, Lil Beeskep.
GEORGE	Absolutely!
LIL	*(Firmly.)* Well! If you ask me, wha' I think we need is… a dance. *(All'improvviso: 'Well, tha's a thought. A dance! A dance at a time like this! Etc.')*

Music 15 – begins. Jack & Wilf enter to play the music.)

	(Sings.) Well, it in't no use complainin';
	It's like moanin' when it's rainin'!
	There in't no point in won'ts or can'ts or shan'ts,
	'Cause wha' will be is gonna be,
	An' wha' we'll see we're gonna see.
	So, what I think we need is a dance. *(Grabs hold of George & makes him dance. Alf grabs, Dora. All'improvviso.)*
	We'll invite all the boys.
	We won't be shy; we won't be coy.
	We'll wrap 'em in our arms 'til their entranced!
GEORGE	*(Laughs.)* Steady on, Lil Beeskep!
LIL	We'll swing 'em round and round
	And whisper lovin' sounds.

	Yes, what I think we need is a dance.
DORA	*(Frees herself & dusts herself down. George & Lil continue to dance.)* Time to go, I think! *(Strides out.)*
ALF	*(Laughs.)* Ay, wait for me, Dora! I'll walk you 'ome!
DORA	No you won't! *(Exits with Alf in pursuit.)*
GEORGE	*(Calls after him.)* Tha's a boy, Alf!
LIL	D'you remember the first war, George? When you was called up. We 'ad a dance in the village 'all. D'you remember? We was so young an' innocent! An' it were such fun! It were a wrench though, watchin' you go. *(Sighs.)*

    'Cause if the boys are goin' away,
    Like swallows, anyday

The play goes back in time for a moment. They hug. He picks up his case, salutes her & leaves. She waves after him.

    (Speaks.) Bye, George! Take care.
        (T'maybe) fall like brittle leaves at Autumn time,
        We'll need to give 'em smiles
        An kisses for a while
        An' 'old 'em in our lovin' arms entwined.
        Yes! We'll invite all of the boys.
        (Repeat verse 2.)

(Speaks.) Well, at least he come back.

Briony runs in with Hugo & a second airman (Biffy).

BRIONY	Hello everybody! Isn't this fun! Hoots in abundance! This is Hugo end Biffy.
HUGO	*(Takes Lil's hand & flirts.)* Well, hello.
LIL	Charmed, I'm sure!
BIFFY	Twiffic!
LIL	Well, come on in, boys! *(They go straight into a dance.)* There's beer at the bar and Marge 'as done all these cakes! They all gotta be eaten, mind. *(All'improvviso: 'Twiffic! I say! Etc.')* I'll go an' get the sandwiches. *(Exits.)*
JACK	*(While playing.)* Briony! Beastly, what! *(He sulks.)*
BRIONY	Oh, don't be a spoil sport Jack! You know, it is so nice to have you boys in the village! Joy in abundance!
HUGO	Really?
BIFFY	Twiffic!
HUGO	Just gort in. Good t'take a breather. *(Flirtatious.)* Pretty gells! A few beers. What! Listen t'the birds twitter rather. Hear m'self think for a while, dash it! *(Gloomy for a moment.)* Been bloody, recent weeks, course.
BRIONY	*(Can't take her eyes off him.)* Oh! Horrors maximus
HUGO	Last operation, bandit came up m'rear.

69

	Spooked me rather. Arse end Charlie took a packet. Biffy here had to bail out. Dint'cha, Biffy?
BIFFY	Warther.
HUGO	Had t'put m'kite down in the drink, wouldn't yuh know. Both of us swam back to Blighty, course. Took a few Jerrys with me, mind.
BRIONY	*(Gone now.)* Oh! You are so brave.

The dance continues. Gertie enters.

GERTIE	*(Enters.)* Gosh! Sorry I'm late.
BRIONY	Oh, Gertie, chum. You came! You came! This is Biffy.
BIFFY	Twiffic! *(Grabs her & starts dancing with her.)*
GERTIE	Hello, Biffy. *(But looking at Jack.)*
BRIONY	And this is Hugo.
HUGO	Well, hello. *(Briony frowns at him, then forces his attention back on her.)*
GERTIE	Hello, Hugo. *(Still looking at Jack.)* Hello Wilf. Hello Jack. *(Jack looks very sulky.)*

One more fast exhilarating verse, then the dance ends.

Music 15 – ends.

BRIONY	Oh! Isn't this wonderful.
GERTIE	Rather!

BRIONY	I could dance all night. *(Dances on.)* Thet nasty Hitler just over the sea barking like a miserable little dog end us all snug'n'warm in our cosy village hall with the cheps keeping us safe! Ohhh! *(She gives Hugo a big hug.)*
JACK	I say, Briony! You... you're... cooing again. *(She lets go of Hugo immediately.)*
BRIONY	*(Huffy.)* Well! We're not engaged! Besides... *(Slightly embarrassed, but with a slight grin becoming coy & glancing at Hugo)* I wasn't. Not much.
JACK	Yes you were, dash it! With... with... him! *(Points at Hugo.)*
HUGO	*(Smirking.)* I say, you're not a weasel are you?
WILF	Now! Now! In't no need f'tha'!
BIFFY	*(Smirking equally.)* I think he is! Twiffic!
JACK	What?
HUGO	It's just you sounded like a weasel.
JACK	What d'yuh mean? No I didn't.
HUGO	Sounded weaselly t'me.
JACK	I say! That's not cricket!
BRIONY	*(Upset now.)* Oh, cheps! Don't let's fight! Please. Not with the war on end the cheps all set to fly out any day!
GERTIE	Well, you were cooing, Briony! End you may not be engaged, but you *did* call Jack your grumpy little badger!
BRIONY	Gertie!

JACK	Thank you, Gertie, ol' girl. The truth is the chep's a… bounder!
HUGO	*(Still smirking. Takes out a cigarette.)* I say! Steady on.
WILF	Tha's enough, Jack!
BIFFY	Shall I biff him, Wingco?
HUGO	Better not, Biffy. On a sticky wicket, rather. Don't want to upset the brass hats. Time t'go, I think. Poor form, though. *(He and Biffy begin to leave. They each flick their cigarette ends at him as they leave.)*
BIFFY	Warther!
BRIONY	Please don't go. *(They leave.)* Hugo! Ohh! End I was having such a good time. Oh! Beastly, Jack! End you, Gertie – End I thought you were my very best friend! Hugo! Wait! *(Runs out.)*
JACK	Briony! Dash it! *(Starts to go but Gertie grabs his arm.)*
GERTIE	Jack! Wait!
JACK	*(Not listening.)* What?
WILF	Oh dear! *(Glares at Jack.)* That's all we wan'! Hugo! *(Runs out)*
GERTIE	Just wait please, Jack. Please. *(Slightly flirtatious.)* Chum. I… I wanted to talk to you, you see. In fect, I wanted to talk to you… very much. *(Fixes him in her gaze.)* Well… the thing is, you don't… *hev* to chase after her, you know. When she runs orf like thet with cheps. You

	could just… let her go. She was awfully frightful after all. End there are… other gells! Nice gells. Not thet Briony isn't nice, you understand. She really *(Pronounce it as rarely)* is awfully nice. End my very best friend. But… what I wanted to say was, there *are*… other gells who would be tirribly considerate to a chep over such a beastly thing as… cooing.
JACK	What? *(Still not listening.)* I… er… Briony! *(Runs out.)*
GERTIE	Jack! Oh! Consternation in abundance! *(Stomps out.)*

CANO 12

A PHONE CALL – *The post office.*
George (M2), Alf (M4), Dora (F1) & Lil (F2)

GEORGE   *(Enters as a phone rings.)* Dring dring! Dring dring! *(Etc. Picks up the phone.)* Jevington three one five. Yes. *(Pause.)* Yes. *(Pause.)* Yes. *(Pause.)* No. This is the post office. *(Pause.)* Yes. Wha'? Yes, Jevington Post Office. I was jus' standin' in for Lil. She's... Wha'? *(Pause.)* No, it in't the police station. Tha's Polegate one 'undred. Yuh need t'speak to Alf. PC Wood. I 'spect 'e'll be poppin' in presently. 'E gen'rally cycles up about this time for a cuppa tea. An' 'oo am I speakin' to? *(Pause.)* Wha'? *(Pause.)* I'll write tha' down. *(Writes down.)* 'A... concerned... member... of... the public.' Yes. *(Alarmed.)* Wha'? Yuh found wha'? *(Pause.)* No! Where? *(Pause.)* In the stream by the church? *(Pause.)* An' yuh say there were two... sparrars? I'll write tha' down. *(Writes.)* 'Two sparrars. S...P...A...R...R...A... R...S.'

Alf enters with Lil.

'Ang on a minute. PC Wood's jus walked in. It's f'you, Alf. *(Gives him the phone.)*

ALF	'Allo? Yes. *(Pause.)* Yes. *(Pause.)* Yes. *(Pause.)* No. This is the post office. *(Pause.)*
LIL	*(Whispers.)* Wha's goin' arf, George? *(He gestures impatiently for her to be quiet.)*
ALF	Yes, this is PC Wood. *(Pause.)* An' yuh found wha'? *(Alarmed.)* Wha'! Where? *(Pause.)* The stream by the church? *(Pause.)* An' yuh say there were two… sparrars? You stay righ' where you are, madam. You did righ' t'report it. This is indeed a very serious ma'er. I'll be righ' up. Ta-ta. *(Dramatic. Puts the phone down.)*
LIL	Wha's goin' arf, Alf?
ALF	*(Serious.)* The Super in't goin' t'like this. *(Writing in his notebook. Dora enters.)*
LIL	Wha'?
DORA	Ah! PC Wood. *(Grinning.)* And what is the Superintendant not going to like?
ALF	*(Dramatic.)* There's bin a body found in the stream by the church.
LIL, GEORGE & DORA	A body! *(All'improvviso.)*
ALF	Not an 'ooman. A swan.
LIL	*(Sighs with relief. All'improvviso: 'A swan! That's a different ma'er. Etc.')* A swan! I thought you meant an 'ooman! Tha' in't quite so…
ALF	Bu' i' is serious, this is! They're royal

	birds, they is. *An'* it looks like foul play! Swans are protected by the crown. It's treason to kill a swan. An' that's a capital offence. It's like threatenin' the King himself! An' tha's very serious. 'Specially in war time. The Super in't goin' t'like this at all.
GEORGE	Oh, it don' surprise me one bit.
DORA	*(Shocked.)* I see. Goodness. Goodness me.
LIL	I'll go and fetch, Wilf. 'E's strong. 'E'll 'elp you with it, Alf.
ALF	Thank you, Lil. *(She exits.)* It were a concerned member of the public, yuh see, 'oo rang in – an' she say tha'… *(Dramatic)* it were jus' layin' there on its side 'alf under water with an' 'ole in its neck as if a butcher's skewer 'ad bin thrust clean through, with its eyes cold an' 'ard an' yellow like stones!
DORA	Gracious!
ALF	*An'* another curious thing. There were two sparrars sittin' on a branch nearby jus' lookin' at it… sad like, as if they'd lorst their mother… *(Pause)* 'cept it were a male swan. Terrible! A terrible thing.
DORA	*(Dramatic pause, then.)* Gypsies!
ALF	No, it in't no use…
GEORGE	Might be, Alf. They're always sniffin' round my yard lookin' f'things t'nick.

ALF	No. C'mon, George. It in't no use jumpin' t'conclusions. It could've bin anybody. The black market. The stuff some people are sellin' under the counter.
DORA	Disgraceful!
GEORGE	You're right there Dora.
ALF	A nazi spy parachuted in in one of these night raids… *or* a fifth columnist trying to undermine our morale! There's all sorts goin' arf, I'll tell you. Well, I can't 'ang about gossipin' with you. I be'er ge' up there an' sort it out. *(Begins to leave.)*
GEORGE	Yes, you go, Alf; we won' keep yuh.
ALF	*(Shaking his head.)* The Super in't gonna like this. 'E in't gonna like this at all. *(Exits.)*

Music 16 – begins

DORA	*(Shaking her head.)* Oh dear! Oh dear, oh dear, oh dear! *(Takes her purse out.)* I'll have two stamps, Mr Beeskep, and a quarter of those mints.
GEORGE	Righ' you are, Mrs Pentlow. *(He gives her the stamps, weighs the mints & gives them to her. Vsfx as he serves her. She puts a mint in her mouth.)*
DORA	Oh dear! Oh dear, oh dear, oh dear! *(Exits, sucking the sweet. George locks the door, shakes his head & exits.)*

CANO 13

A HOST OF SPARROWS – The hedgerow.
Peter Sparrow (M1) & Pegotty Sparrow (F2)

Music 16 – ends.

> *Pegotty Sparrow flies in. Through her body language & tone of voice she suggests she has her seven babies with her. She is anxious & stressed. From time to time she pulls a worm out of the ground or picks up grubs & feeds them to her babies.*

PEGOTTY Fancy! Come 'ere! Fern! Hazel, Rupert! Eat yuh worms. Oh, dear! Oh, dear! Wha' are we t'do? Edward! Acorn! Will you stop fightin'! Beaks are for eating with. 'Ow many times 'ave I told you tha'? Not pecking each other! An' get out of the nest, Simon! You know we can't all get in together. Yes, Fern; I did promise you a song. In a minute, Rupert! Now let me see. *(Thinks what to sing.)* Edward, yuh can eat the red ones, but the green ones will give you a tummy ache. I've told you tha'. Yes, yes. That's alright. Now are you listenin'?

Music 17 – begins.

> *(Sings.)* Babies come roundly,
> Come roundly, come round,
> Up daisy, down daisy,
> Babies come round.

When the sun's sunny,
When cuckoo calls –
Cuckoo! Sweet cuckoo! –
When cuckoo calls –

(When) beetles an' gnats fly
An' bugs come a-crawlin'
Tuck away! Tuck away!
Feast all the mornin'.
Feast on the worms
An' the moths an' the flies,
Bu' don't touch the 'oney bee.
Stay clear of 'er 'ive!

(An' when) pussycat's comin'
On softly soft paws
Fly away! Fly away!
Flee from 'is claws!
An' when the wind's blowin',
When the dark moans,
Listen for mama
An' quickly fly 'ome –

An' when the moon's callin'
An' the night yawns *(She yawns)*,
When pixies frolic with
Satyrs and fauns,
It's time to be sleepin'
At 'ome in your nest.
So come 'ome to mama.
Come 'ome to rest.

Music 17 – ends.

Peter Sparrow flies in & perches on a branch nearby.

PEGOTTY Pe'er! You're back! *(To her children.)* Now, you lot! Out of the nest an' amuse yuhselves for a while. I gotta talk to yuh Pa. Go on! Shoo! An' Edward, don' eat the green ones! D'yuh 'ear? *(To Peter.)* Pe'er! Wha's 'appenin'? Did yuh see anythin'?

PETER *(Very anxious.)* 'Oomans 'ave took the body away. An' all the birds – the coots, an' the 'erons an' the geese an' all – are jus' standin around like poor lost souls!

PEGOTTY An' what abou' 'er majesty?

PETER They took 'er away, too, in a crate with bars like she's goin' orf to gaol – an' she jus' standin' there like a ghost moanin' an' moanin' sof'ly like she's mad or somethin'!

PEGOTTY Oh, Pe'er! Wha' we gonna do?

PETER I don' think no-one seen us Peg. Least, I don' think so.

PEGOTTY *(Whispers.)* Bu' we did see i', din't we?

PETER *(Looking round nervously.)* Ssshh! Don't….!

PEGOTTY Bu' we saw…You know! Wha' we saw! 'Is… Macbyrd's… the raven! 'Is beak nestled against the swan's neck like an 'ooman babe at the breast! Then 'im

	cawin' an' cawin' an' cryin' out like 'e's bin… pecked. Black an' white feathers all tumblin' t'gether an' 'im desperate t' fly away. We did see i', din't we? We did, din't we?
PETER	Yes. We saw i' alright.
PEGOTTY	Bu' wha' should we do? Shouldn't we tell someone?
PETER	*(Adamant.)* No! 'Ow can we? 'Oo're we gonna tell? 'Oo's gonna believe us? We in't nobody! Just… sparrows. An' 'e's big an' powerful an' silky an' sleek! A raven. *An'* 'e's the mayor! Nobody in't gonna believe us. They might even blame us! 'Cause we was there.
PEGOTTY	Wha'! No! Surely? Not us. Sparrows? We couldn't do nothin'. We're too small!
PETER	Bu' they're gonna need someone. To blame. Don't yuh see? Someone… small. Someone 'oo can be stood on. A li'le 'andful of feathers like us. 'Oo don' ma'er!
PEGOTTY	Oh! Pe'er! Wha' we gonna do?
PETER	Look! Don't you worry, Pegotty. 'S'long as nobody's seen us, we'll be alright. C'mon!

Music 18 – begins.

PEGOTTY	I 'ope so. *(He holds her tenderly for a moment.)* Fancy! Fern! Hazel! Rupert! Acorn! Edward! Simon! Quickly! Time t' fly! *(They fly out.)*

CANO 14

ALMOST LOVERS – *The manor & the cricket field.*
Hugo (M2), Jack (M3), Briony (F1) & Gertie (F2)

Music 18 – ends.

BRIONY (*She enters as Hugo comes the other way.*) Oh! Hugo. It's you!

She's quite gone on him by now.

HUGO (*Pleased to see her.*) Hello, Briony.
BRIONY I do so hope dinner was alright.
HUGO Yes, it was. Splendid! Quite splendid.
BRIONY Mummy end deddy are delighted to have you end the cheps here in the manor, you know. In fect, kent imagine what it was like before you came.
HUGO Really?
BRIONY And it is alright for us up in the attic. In fect, it's quite snug really.
HUGO Really? I am so pleased.
BRIONY End I still have my very own room. It's just along there, in fect, end… up… there… (*Embarrassed for a moment*).
HUGO I see. Oh, look! Through the window. There's a moon! How lovely!
BRIONY Yes, how perfectly lovely! It's pink! D'you see how pink it is? A grapefruit moon.
HUGO Yes, it is! How perfectly…

BRIONY	*(Looks at him.)* Romantic!
HUGO	*(Pause.)* Briony! *(Takes her hand & examines it.)* You know, it is… bloody up there for us cheps!
BRIONY	I know!
HUGO	With Jerry constantly at our tail or on our becks. *(He glances around anxiously with his eyes only as if he might be under attack any minute.)* End t'know there's a gell back in Blighty waiting for us to come home. *(Slowly.)* To feel the silky smoothness of a dress, or the softness of a… woolly jumper, or the warmth of a gell's skin! It is… a comfort, you know!
BRIONY	*(Looking into his eyes.)* Yes, I know, Hugo. End a gell does want to be here for you.
HUGO	Yes. *(They move to kiss, but then spring apart as Biffy enters.)*
BIFFY	I say! Twiffic gwub warther!
HUGO	Hello, Biffy. *(Briony is now looking intently out of the window.)*
BIFFY	You cheps coming down for'wa snifter? Just the ticket I should think!
HUGO	Good thinking, Biffy. *(Makes to go.)*
BRIONY	*(Still looking out of the window.)* D'you know I think thet's Jack darn there on the cricket field with… with… Gertie.
BIFFY	Come on ol' gell. *(They go with Briony still looking out of the window until she*

	finally pulls herself away.)
GERTIE	*(Jack enters followed by Gertie. Earnest.)* So you're… going away!
JACK	*(Slightly distracted.)* What? Yes. Gort m'papers this morning. Travers brought them up with m'boiled egg and toasted soldiers. *(Gazing at the wicket.)* Wicket looks splendid. Max mowed it 'specially, y'know.
GERTIE	*(Sensitive.)* Gort you middle stump, I should think.
JACK	Yes. Turning… wicket… rather.
GERTIE	Googly, I expect?
JACK	Yes. *(Pause. Thoughtful.)* Royal Sussex.
GERTIE	The Royal Sussex Regiment?
JACK	No. Golf Club. Only applied last week. Gort m'membership.
GERTIE	*(Upset.)* Oh, Jack! End I thought…!
JACK	*(Paying attention finally.)* Gertie! I say! You're not…?
GERTIE	*(Recovers.)* Blubbing! Yes, I am! So there. End I am so tirribly sorry.
JACK	*(Pause.)* You weren't… blubbing, 'cause I'm going away, were you?
GERTIE	*(Ernest.)* But are you going away? Are you?
JACK	Yes! Course. All the cheps are. Didn't yuh know? As I said. Gort m'papers this morning. Intelligence Corps. London. Hush hush apparently. Something called the SOE. Desk job, probably.

GERTIE	But the golf club? You said…
JACK	Yes, Just thinking… *(Thoughtful for a moment)* a chep might get a green in before I… I say, Gertie, ol' thing! If you were… blubbing…'cause of jolly ol' me, does that mean?
GERTIE	*(Pause.)* Does it mean what, Jack?
JACK	Well… you know, ol'gell.
GERTIE	*(Braces herself. Slowly.)* If you mean… thet a chep is asking a gell whether she has… feelings for a chep under this… *(They gaze up at the moon)* perfectly… romantic moon, then… I hope you don't mind my saying thet… I do.
JACK	*(Long pause.)* Golly! B…b…but, Gertie, I… I… didn't know.
GERTIE	You see all I am is just… Briony's very best friend. The gell who admires her dress end shares her secrets, while *she* gets the…. cheps… like you. I don't mind! I really don't. I *am* her very best friend. But… I do know how to love, you see.
JACK	*(Stares at her. Another long pause. Then)* Golly! Oh! Gertie! *(Grabs her & kisses her passionately on the lips.)*
GERTIE	*(Fighting to get him off.)* Jack! Get… orf! *(Looking round in case someone is watching.)* Someone might be watching! *(Pushes him away & brushes herself down.)*

85

JACK But… but…

Music 19 – begins.

GERTIE *(Grabs his hand & drags him off.)* Come on! Let's just walk for a while, shell we? *(They exit.)*

CANO 15

A NEW ERA – *The oak tree.*
Feather (M1), Inspector Seed (M2), Macbyrd (M3), Quill (M4), Bertha Coot & Wormwood (F1) & Rosebud Coot (F2)

Music 19 – ends.

> *Feather enters followed by Inspector Seed, a pigeon, & Quill.*

FEATHER	This way!
SEED	*(Writes in his notebook.)* 'Oppin', you say?
FEATHER	Yes, Inspector Seed. Hopping! Always hopping.
SEED	And… *(Writes)* leavin'… their… deposits?
QUILL	Oh! You don't know what trouble we have with the crows, Inspector! There never used to be so many, you know. Flying in here! Taking over the lake! Hopping about!
FEATHER	And the magpies are worse! Gypsies! Gypsies!
SEED	*(Writes)* Gyp…sies.
QUILL	It used to be such a pleasant…
FEATHER	And the moorhens! Strutting and pecking their heads! *(Demonstrates.)* Getting above their station!
QUILL	*(Dubious.)* Yerrs.
FEATHER	*And* the sparrows! They wanted to nest…

QUILL	…in the willows! No wonder there's trouble! I could see it coming. I really could.
FEATHER	*(Distressed.)* And now… the lake! Gone! Gone!
QUILL	What *are* we to do?
FEATHER	*(Looking off.)* Look out! They're here!

Macbyrd & Wormwood fly in & settle on a branch.

QUILL & FEATHER	*(They bow deeply.)* Your worshipful! *(To Seed.)* Macbyrd, Inspector Seed.
MACBYRD	Ah, Seed. You've come. Terrible business. Terrible.
QUILL	The mayor. *(Gesturing to him.)* Such a… tower of strength! (*All'improvviso: 'Tower of strength!'*)
MACBYRD	Nah, nah, nah! Tha's enough. Tha's enough.
FEATHER	A leader! A born leader! I always said so.
QUILL	In difficult times. There is always one. Who… will… rise…
FEATHER	…to the occasion.
WORMWOOD	*(To Macbyrd.)* Yuh see! Yuh see! *(Gesturing to them.)*
MACBYRD	*(In his element. Oratorical. Gradual crescendo.)* Times 'ave changed, yuh see, Inspector Seed. An' change… is… difficult. *(All'improvviso: 'It ain't easy.')* For the… administration. *(Gestures*

	to Quill & Feather. All'improvviso: 'Admin.') For the… police. *(Gestures to Seed. All'improvviso: 'The old bill.')* For the populace at large. *(Gestures widely.)*
WORMWOOD	Tha's you's lot. *(Gestures to the audience.)*
MACBYRD	An' indeed for the leaders. *(Gestures to himself & Wormwood. She straightens up, emotional with pride.)* The lake…'as gone! *(All'improvviso: 'Iss gone.')* Bu' the oak tree *(Gestures to it)*… is still 'ere. *(All'improvviso: 'The oak tree! The oak tree!')* Our beloved ruler, Cygnus, an' 'is delightful Pen are sadly no more *(General shaking of heads, etc. All'improvviso, 'Terrible! Terrible!).* But… Macbyrd is 'ere – an' 'e… I…will fill the void. *(All'improvviso: Macbyrd! Macbyrd!')* The wa'er may 'ave gone, bu' we still 'ave the sky. *(Louder all'improvviso: 'The sky! The sky!')* The beau'y an' elegance of the swan may 'ave 'ad its demise… Bu'! The silky an' sleek blackness of the raven… *(All'improvviso: The raven! The raven!')* will rise into the azure blue! White! 'As… become… black, so t'speak. *(They start chanting: White black! Black white! White black! Black white! Etc.)* It's jus' change! Tha's all.Change! *(Gradually the chanting becomes a cacophony of quacking & squawking.)*

SEED	Wait! Wait! Macbyrd! All of you! Stop! *(They stop instantly when Macbyrd shouts at them to shut up.)* Don't you see! All this is well an' good. Everyfin' in its place. Bu'! Don' you understand? *(Slowly.)* There's bin… a murder! An' we don' know 'oo done it. *(General, if quiet & slightly embarrassed, agreement. All'improvviso: 'Yeh. Of course. That's right. Etc.')*
MACBYRD	*(Slightly on the back foot but recovers quickly.)* Yes. You… are… of course quite righ', Seed. All in good time. Everyfin' in its place, so t'speak. Bu'… we also 'ave, in these troubled times…
WORMWOOD	*(Half whispered.)* Tell 'im! Go on! Tell 'im!
MACBYRD	Yeh, alrigh'! Alrigh'! Bu'… in these difficult days… we've gotta fink abou'… order! Securi'y. The safety of the public. The populace need t'fly in safety. We don' wan' chaos! We don' wan' the state t'fall apart!
SEED	Yes, bu'…
WORMWOOD	Tell 'im!

They all look backwards & forwards between Macbyrd & Wormwood. Gripped. All'improvviso: 'What? What is it? Etc.

MACBYRD	Well, as a ma'er of fact, I do 'ave some

	information tha' may, as it 'appens… appertain to this ma'er.
SEED	Go on! Go on!
MACBYRD	I was flyin'… on the evenin' of the… er… murder, up above, 'igh up. I do sometimes. Fly… 'igh up. T'be able to breathe. T'feel the light. *(There is a brief moment of conscience, but he soon recovers.)* An' there was a… a… foreigner. *(All'improvviso: 'A foreigner! I knew it! Etc.)*
FEATHER	I knew all along it would be a foreigner! They're always trouble!
QUILL	Trouble! You're right! Always trouble!
SEED	Bu' wha' kind of foreigner, Macbyrd?
MACBYRD	*(Trying to remember.)* A… Professor Bhatta… Butta… Bitta… I can' remember. Bu' 'e was a lark! *(All'improvvso echoing Macbyrd's words.)*
SEED	A lark! Bu' surely, Macbyrd? A li'le fing like tha'! A li'le bundle of feathers like tha'? Kill… a swan?
FEATHER	Well, you say that, but you can never tell with foreigners.
QUILL	He's right, you know. All manner of tricks they have. Up their sleeves!
FEATHER	Black arts some of 'em!
MACBYRD	I ain't sayin' nothin'! Except… I know… wha' I saw!
SEED	Well, yes. Thank you. I'll make a note of it. *(Writes.)* A… foreigner.

FEATHER	Quite right.
MACBYRD	Shuddup! *(Feather instantly drops into an obsequious posture.)*
SEED	Fank you, Macbyrd. All information is… er… relevant at this moment in time. I will call on you again if I may. *(Macbyrd nods & Seed flies out.)*
MACBYRD	*(He yells at Quill & Feather.)* Go on! Get out! *(They fly out.)*

Macbyrd's head drops into a slough of despondency.

Music 20 – begins.

WORMWOOD	*(Grips his arm.)* Listen! Listen! You've gotta 'ave courage! You did righ'! It's righ' 'e's gone! *(Slowly.)* Think of the sparrows. The wrens. 'E din't care about them! 'E din't care about the birds! 'E was a fish! A cold ferocious fish! Rippin' their li'le innocent 'earts out! Yuh said so yuhself. You did righ'. You're an 'ero. A leader. You gotta lead *them* now. You… *did*… right! It's *your* time now. Tha's wha' the magpies said! Din't they? *(He pulls away from her and flies out. Calls after him.)* Tha's wha' they said! Courage, Macbyrd! Courage! *(To herself.)* Courage. *(She flies out.)*

CANO 16

A LETTER FOR HUGO – *The same.*
Hugo (M2) & Briony (F1)

Music 20 – ends.

BRIONY (*Excited. To the audience.*) A letter. (*Shows them.*) It's for Hugo. (*Reads.*) Wing Commander Hugo Ffinch-Hatton, C/o The Post Office, Jevington, Sussex. (*She hugs it as if it is him & sighs.*) I was at the post office end Mrs Beeskep asked me to deliver it to him. He's staying at the Manor, you see. All the cheps are. (*Gazes at it. Slowly.*) End she asked to make sure I delivered it right into his… hends. His lovely soft hends with their pretty pink nails with little moons for cuticles. (*Sighs again.*) It's probably tirribly important. Special instructions, or something. (*Pause. A cloud descends for a moment.*) Unless it's from a gell. I expect gells are always falling for him. Someone… like… him. So lovely end so brave. (*She sniffs it.*) Doesn't smell as though it's from a gell, though. Could be from his mother, I suppose. His dear lovely mama! She probably wanted to write before he started his new mission. With him

	maybe… *(Another cloud)* not… coming… beck! I expect she's very proud of him. A mother would be. End anxious, too, of course! *(Pause. Gazes at it again.)* I think… he likes me. He did kiss me! Well, nearly *(Say it like rarely)* – and I think I… love him! I have this feeling, you see, right here. *(Gestures.)* A dizzy, fizzing, sort of falling feeling like drinking champagne, or like… the moment a rose suddenly pops open from a bud, end perfume floats in tiny drops into the air! *(Pause.)* He might ask me to be his wife! I *would* love his children – Our children! – in their little keps end blazers… end I would kiss them end send them orf to school with their bags end tuck end tell them not to worry about matron because she really would be a good sort in the end end not spank them. End I would wait for him at the door in my pinny end… end hear him coming up the path end open the door end he would be there end say…
HUGO	*(Enters in her fantasy.)* Briony, darling! You know, it was… bloody up there for us today! End it's such a comfort to know you will be here!
BRIONY	*(To the audience.)* End I would fetch his slippers.
HUGO	Slippers.

BRIONY	*(He sits & she puts his slippers on him.)* I heard from the boys.
HUGO	Did you? Did you really? End has matron been quite so beastly? Sherry.
BRIONY	*(She gets his sherry.)* Not quite, I think – end they *do* seem to be having terrific fun in the dorm with midnight feasts end things. *(To the audience.)* End I *would* be so tirribly heppy to bring his sherry.
HUGO	*(Stands up & lights his pipe.)* You know, darling, bringing m'kite home over Beachy Head this morning I was struck with how beautiful England is.
BRIONY	Oh, yes! *(They simultaneously become a spitfire & fly around the stage.)*
HUGO	Look! 9.00 o'clock. *(They change their gaze to 9.00 o'clock.)* The wheat end barley waving in the breeze like a mother's hend through a child's hair. End a Southdowns bus scurrying along a winding lane like a busy little green beetle. End at 3.00 o'clock. Look! *(Their gaze changes again.)* Across the Darns as the slope dips sharply into the clays end greensand of the Weald the fields laid out like pocket hendkerchiefs sewn together with dirty cotton. You see, it is so tirribly… tirribly…lovely.
BRIONY	Yes, my darling! I see it! *(Slowly.)* So tirribly… tirribly…lovely!

HUGO	*(They come into land.)* Weeeeeooooowww! *(The fantasy ends suddenly.)*
BRIONY	*(Surprised to see him.)* Oh, Hugo. *(She glances at the letter & then hides it behind her back.)*
HUGO	*(Slightly embarrassed to see her.)* Ah! Briony. Didn't see you at breakfast.
BRIONY	No. Gort up early. I was walking Nippy, my Scottie. You've probably seen him.
HUGO	Ah, yes. Chippy… little fellah.
BRIONY	*(Pause.)* Lovely… moon last night.
HUGO	Yes, splendid.
BRIONY	*(Pause.)* It was nice to… chet.
HUGO	Rather. *(Uncomfortable silence for a moment.)* Well. Must… get orf.
BRIONY	Yes. *(Pause.)* Take care, won't you?
HUGO	Rather. *(Turns and strides out.)*

Music 21 – begins.

BRIONY	*(Takes the letter out from behind her back. Looks at it.)* I'll just… keep it. Just… for a little while longer, I think. *(Thoughtul. Hugs the letter, then runs out.)*

CANO 17

THE COOTS BRING NEWS – *The same.*
Feather (M1), Inspector Seed (M2), Macbyrd (M3), Quill (M4), Bertha Coot (F1) & Rosebud Coot (F2)

Music 21 – ends.

MACBYRD	*(Macbyrd flies in followed by Quill & Feather.)* Bu'…. not the sparrows! Such tiny li'le fings. Jus' bundles of fevvers. *(To the audience.)* No weight at all in an 'ooman 'and.
FEATHER	But, if I may say so, your worshipful, you did… let them…
QUILL	…nest in the willows.
FEATHER	Contrary to our advice.
QUILL	And, sure as not, when you make concessions to the…
FEATHER	Common classes…
QUILL	The populace.
FEATHER	…then the base instincts *will* come out.
QUILL	Pride!
FEATHER	Ambition!
QUILL	Wanting to rise above their natural station!
FEATHER	The swan knew. He understood.
QUILL	Breed less! He said.
FEATHER	Cygnus showed them their rightful place, you see…
QUILL	He showed them!

FEATHER	… so they had…
QUILL	*(Dramatic)* …the motive!
MACBYRD	Bu'… sparrows!
FEATHER	*(Slowly.)* But they were seen.
MACBYRD	What!
QUILL	Near the body.
FEATHER	On a branch. Dark, brooding eyes!
QUILL	Blood… on… their claws!
FEATHER	Lustful for revenge!
QUILL	Sitting there, calm and cold.
FEATHER	Staring! Into the swan's stony… silent… dead… yellow… eyes.

Macbyrd turns away. Animated, almost laughing. Almost demented. He's off the hook.

MACBYRD	*(To himself.)* They was there! They was seen! An' they never saw me. An' they 'ad a motive! I'm aright. I'm alright. I'm gonna be… al…right.
SEED	*(Enters.)* Macbyrd. *(Macbyrd swings round surprised.)*
MACBYRD	Ah! Seed! Inspector Seed. You're 'ere. Tha's… good.
SEED	I understan' there's bin a development.
MACBYRD	Yes. A…development. There are… witnesses.
SEED	Witnesses?
FEATHER	The Coots!
MACBYRD	*(To himself.)* The Coots!
QUILL	Rosebud and Bertha Coot. Sisters.

SEED	*(Writes in his book.)* Rose… bud… an' Ber…fa… Coot.
FEATHER	*(Half to himself.)* Busybodies. *(Their heads pop round the scenery.)*
QUILL	*(In quick. Glares at Feather.)* Highly respected! Ladies from the community. They saw the suspects…
FEATHER	Vicious little brutes!
QUILL	…standing over the body!
FEATHER	With blood on their claws!
SEED	*(Writes. Shaking his head.)* Blood! Oh, dear. Dear dear me! Dear dear me!
QUILL	We have them here, Inspector. Just outside.
MACBYRD	Then bring them in! Bring them in!
FEATHER	*(Goes to fetch them.)* Miss Rosebud and Miss Bertha! *(They enter instantly.)*
MACBYRD	Ah! The Coots! Come in! Come in! Rosebud and… er…
QUILL	Bertha.
MACBYRD	Bertha! We understan' you 'ave… information. Come on! Tell the inspector! Tell the inspector!
SEED	Ahem! *(Glares discretely at Macbyrd.)* Ladies. I understan' you are…?
ROSEBUD	Rosebud …
BERTHA	…and Bertha Coot.
TOGETHER	Miss. Quwark!
ROSEBUD	You know, we did love their royalnesses! I met them, you know!
BERTHA	She took their photograph.

ROSEBUD	Ardent supporters, we were.
BERTHA	They were so…!
SEED	Yes! Fank you. Now, I believe you saw somefink?
ROSEBUD	*(With real ferocity.)* The common little brutes!
BERTHA	We knew there would be trouble.
ROSEBUD	The hedgerows used to be so lovely…
BERTHA	…before *they* moved in!
SEED	Bu' 'oo, ladies? 'Oo?
ROSEBUD	The sparrows, of course!
BERTHA	Swarming all over the place…
ROSEBUD	…with their little brats…!
SEED	*(Patiently impatient.)* Bu' wha' did you see, ladies?
BERTHA	Oh! *(Becomes distraught.)* It was there…
ROSEBUD	The body! *(She's distraught now.)* His lovely… white body!
BERTHA	…laying…dead! In the stream.
ROSEBUD	And the sparrows sitting there with… dark… cold… evil eyes… gloating at what they had done.
SEED	Bu'! Did you see blood on their claws?
BERTHA	*(The sisters looking at each other. Confering.)* Well, there was a sunset. Yes, I suppose there was quite a lot of red about. The light and so forth.
ROSEBUD	But it could have been blood. Yes, it definitely could have been blood.
SEED	Bu'!

BERTHA   *(Emphatic.)* There was! It *was* definitely blood!

All'improvviso: 'Blood! There was blood! I knew it! Blood! Blood! Etc.' Quill, Feather & the Coots gradually break into the 'Black white! White black!' chant with it finally evolving again into a cacophony of quacking & squawking.

SEED   *(Trying to be heard. Shouting.)* Bu'… are you sure? Are you sure?
MACBYRD   Shuddup! *(They are all quiet instantly.)*
SEED   Now, fink abart i'! Are you sure? *(Slowly.)* Was there blood on the sparrows' claws?
BERTHA   *(Almost with a bitterness.)* Yes!
ROSEBUD   Definitely! *(Shocked silence.)*
SEED   *(Puts his notebook away.)* Then, I must ask you all t' take the grea'est caution an' not under any circumstances approach the said birds. I 'ave reason t' believe they may be… very… dangerous. An' furvermore, do *not* leave the vicini'y. I will need you to make statements. Fank you. *(Nods to Macbyrd & leaves.)*

Music 22 – begins.

MACBYRD   *(Gestures for the rest to leave. Distressed. Slowly.)* The sparrows. The sparrows. A li'le bundle of fevvers, tha's all. A li'le… bundle of… fevvers. They said it was the sun. 'Cause the sun… painted red… the vale… an' the 'ill. It was the sun… paintin' the leaves an' the branches. The sun! An' the light! *(Looks up at the sky.)* It weren't blood. It was the red… light… of the sun tha' 'ad painted their tiny little claws. An' the babies! Wha's gonna 'appen t' the babies? The li'le bundles of baby fevvers tha' are so light in an 'ooman 'and! *(Looks around disorientated for a moment, then flies off.)*

CANO 18

THE SPARROWS – *Swan Meadow, now an airfield.*
Wilf (M1), Hugo (M2), Biffy (M4) & Briony (F1)

HUGO *(Hugo & Biffy come running in, dressed for flight, followed by Wilf.)* Actions stations, Biffy! *(They are all action as they prepare for flight.)* Whad'yuh say, Biffy? Give Jerry a beating, shall we? *(They climb into their spitfires. Wilf spins Hugo's propeller. The engine bursts into life.)*

BIFFY Twiffic, Wingco! *(Wilf does the same for him.)*

WILF *(Pulls Hugo's chocks.)* Chocks away, Hugo! *(Now Biffy's.)* Chocks away, Biffy!

Hugo & Biffy take off as Briony enters US. Wilf watches them, then exits. Briony enters & watches, too, then waves as they fly out of sight.

BRIONY *(Sings.)* I once heard a sparrow sing in the night.
She sang so pretty in the moonlight.
It made my heart ache; it made my heart sore,
And she sang so pretty when she sang at my door.

(You see) she sang for her gallant who'd flown right away;

Across the ploughed fields, he'd flown far away,
To some distant wood, and it made her heart sore,
But she still sang so pretty when she sang at my door.

She knew he'd be back; she knew he was true,
So she sang to the moon, 'It's a thing he must do.
And I know he'll come back, though it makes my heart sore!'
And she did sing so pretty when she sang at my door.

He'd gone for their babies, to feed them they must
With wrigglies and tigglies and crawlies and crusts.
They were tucked in her nest, huddled two, three and four –
And she sang so pretty when she sang at my door.

(I said) Sleep little sparrows, that's what you must do
Just like other sparrows; they sleep! Yes, they do.
But she sang all the same for her little ones four.

Yes, she sang so pretty when she sang at my door.

He'll come home, yes he will. He'll be home when he's ready
With wrigglies and tigglies and thistles and berries.
There's no need for fretting, yes, it *does make* the heart sore –
Yet she sang so pretty when she sang at my door.

And I looked out to sea above white crashing waves
And I searched and I searched for *my* gallant so brave –
And I hoped he'd come home, back home to our shore –
(And, oh,) she sang so pretty when she sang at my door.
(She exits.)

Music 22 – ends.

Inspector Seed flies in followed by Peter & Pegotty Sparrow harassed in turn by Quill.

SEED	Bring 'em in, Quill! Bring 'em in!
PEGOTTY	*(Distressed.)* Bu' my babies! My babies! There's no-one to feed my babies!
QUILL	You should have thought of that. Oh,

	yes. A bit late now!
SEED	Quill. If you wouldn't mind…
PETER	Bu' we in't done nothin'! We're jus'… sparrows.
QUILL	Oh, yes! That's what they all say! Coming in here with their sob stories! Filling up the hedgerows! Lowering the tone of the…!
SEED	Quill! Would you mind!
PETER	Bu' inspector! I plead wiv you! 'Ow could we 'ave done it? We're too small. Our li'le beaks struggle even wiv a worm. We can 'ardly pull a long wiggly worm out of the ground, let alone….!

Macbyrd flies in. He is strange. Distant & preoccupied.

	Macbyrd! Mayor! You know us. You tried to 'elp us! You know we wouldn't do nothin'!
MACBYRD	*(Not listening.)* It was the sun. The sun… painted red… the vale… an' the 'ill.
PEGOTTY	*(Pleading.)* My babies!
PETER	'Elp us!
SEED	Bu' you was seen! Don' you understand?
PETER	What?
SEED	The Coots! They sin you! You was there! You 'ad blood on your claws!
PETER & PEG	Blood? What? There weren't no…!
MACBYRD	*(In his own world.)* It was the sun. The light.
SEED	Tell me! Were you there, or weren't you?

PETER	*(Afraid to speak. Pause. Drops his head.)* Yes.

Quill starts squawking 'Black white! White black!' 'til it degenerates into manic quacking again with Peter & Pegotty pleading there was no blood & Seed trying to get them all to be quiet.

	Bu' there weren't any blood! There weren't!
SEED	Take them away! *(Quill chases them out, harassing them viciously. All'improvviso: 'You brutes! Come on! My babies! Bu' there weren't no blood! We din't do nothin'! Etc.')*
MACBYRD	*(Still not really paying attention to what is going on.)* It was the sun, yuh see. The sun. It painted red... the vale... an' the 'ill.
SEED	*(Listening to him for the first time.)* Wha'? Wha' did yuh say?
MACBYRD	*(Demented. Manic. Almost laughing.)* They din't do it. 'Ow could they?
SEED	*(Urgent.)* Wha'! Wha' did yuh say?
MACBYRD	Jus' li'le bundles of fevvers in an 'ooman 'and.
SEED	Listen! Wha' are you sayin'?
MACBYRD	I was there! I saw.
SEED	You were there! You saw! Wha' did yuh see? Come on!
MACBYRD	There weren't no blood. Not on them. There was a sunset. It was the sun. The light. It painted their claws red... an'

	the vale… 'an the 'ill.
SEED	So 'oo done it then? 'Oo done it? Did yuh see? Come on!
MACBYRD	*(Slight pause.)* It were me, weren't it! It were me.
SEED	What!

Music 23 – begins.

MACBYRD	They couldn't have done i'! A li'le bundle of fevvers like them!
SEED	Careful wha' you are sayin', Macbyrd!
MACBYRD	'Course it were me! 'E deserved it! 'E din't care about the wrens an' the sparrows! 'Ow could 'e? 'E weren't a bird! Wha' kind of bird was 'e? Poncin' an' preenin'! What did 'e know about sparrows? 'E was a fish! Cold like a fish. *(To the audience.)* 'E should prowl the shadowy bottom with 'is fierce whiskers,'e should! *(Flies out.)*
SEED	'Ere wait a minute! Come back! I in't finished wiv you! Macbyrd! Come back! Oi! Oh, gawd! *(Trying to fly.)* I must lose some weight.

Walks for a moment pecking absurdly with his head, struggling to get into the air because of his fat pigeon body, then eventually flies off after Macbyrd.

Music 23 – ends.

CANO 19

THE AIR & THE LIGHT – *Above the Sussex coast*
Hugo (M2), Macbyrd (M3), Biffy (M4) & Wormwood (F2)

BIFFY (*He flies in.*) Wwwwwwwmmmm! Biffy to contwoller. Looking good. Seems Jewwy's gort his tail between his legs. Twiffic! Turning f'home. Over. Wwwwwooooow! (*He turns for home.*) Biffy again, to contwoller. Can't see Beachy Head. Covered in cloud. Wait a minute! There it is! Up ahead. Just see it peeking thwough. Dashed… beautiful… in the morning light, if I may say so. (*Alters direction.*) Weeeeeooom! And there's the lighthouse! Twiffic! Good to see it, warther! (*Enthusiastic.*) Sticking up out of the cloud, wed an' white like a stick of wock at a candy floss stall. Wipping! Have one of those maybe when we get home. Whad'ya think? Can't see Wingco though. Not seen him for a while, in fact. Must admit. Over. (*Slight pause.*) Biffy to Wingco. Are you weceiving me? Are… you… weceiving me? Over.

HUGO (*He flies in.*) Wwwwwwwooooww! Receiving you loud end clear, Biffy. Over.

BIFFY I see you. Thwee o'clock. (*Urgent.*) I say, Wingo! You've caught a packet! Tail's on fire! Tail's on fire! Over.

HUGO	*(Calm.)* I hear you, Biffy. Jerry copped me from behind, 'fraid. Out of the blue at 6 o'clock. Didn't see 'im. Too close to ditch her though. So gonna try end land it on the deck. Over.
BIFFY	Good luck, sir! *(Urgent.)* Look! I'm wight behind you, Wingco! Take it steady and… the very best… chum! Over.
HUGO	I hear you, Biffy. Over end out. Weeeeeeeoooowwwwm! *(Flies out.)*
BIFFY	Weeeeeeeoooowwwwm! *(Flies out.)*

Macbyrd flies in followed by Wormwood.

WORMWOOD	*(Gasping.)* Wait! Wait! We're too 'igh! Much too 'igh! I can't breave. Where're you goin'? Wait!
MACBYRD	*(He's gasping, too. He's out of his element.)* The light! I gotta get up into the light! There was a lark. I need t'speak to 'im! I need… t'speak… to 'im!
WORMWOOD	Why did yuh tell 'em? Why? You didn' 'ave t'tell 'em.
MACBYRD	I did! The babies! There was no-one t'feed the babies!
WORMWOOD	*(Still gasping.)* Bu' we'll fly away. We'll go somewhere else. Where no-one will find us. We'll be alright! We'll be alright!
MACBYRD	Bu' the sun! *(Gazing up into the sky.)* It

	painted their claws, you see! Red! Their li'le innocent claws!
WORMWOOD	Bu' yuh did right! Listen to me! 'E deserved it! 'E din't care about no babies. 'E was a fish. Yuh said it yuhself. It's your time now.
MACBYRD	It ain't! Don't you see? All they wan'ed was the ring!
WORMWOOD	The ring? Wha' ring?
MACBYRD	The ring from his leg! The silver ring on the swan's leg! They wan'ed it! I seen 'em playin' wiv it!
WORMWOOD	Wha'?
MACBYRD	They like pretty things, don' they? The magpies! So they wan'ed 'im dead! Jus' for a... pretty... li'le ring!
WORMWOOD	*(Not understanding.)* Bu' they said! The magpies said! The time of the swan was over an' tha' it was your time!
MACBYRD	They didn't! They *said!* Dark winged birds would rule meadow an' rye, bu' they weren't talkin' about me! They were talkin' about 'ooman birds! Sleek... an' shiny... an' black against...

Music 24 – begins.

| HUGO | *(Hugo flies in. Everything goes into slow motion. Hits Macbyrd. Wormwood is swept aside by the draft.)* Shuuuuuuurrrrgggh! *(He flies straight out.)* |

Macbyrd goes into free fall, turning & turning as he exits.

WORMWOOD   Macbyrd! *(She flies out after him.)*

Music 24 – ends.

CANO 20

The finale – *Swan Meadow & the garden of Hillside Cottage*
Wilf (M1), Hugo & George (M2), Jack (M3), Alf (M4), Briony (F1) & Gertie & Lil (F2)

Wilf runs in carrying fire buckets. Alf is close behind. Wilf gazes up into the sky.

WILF	Look, Alf! There it is! *(Points up into the sky.)*
ALF	Oh, gawd! *(Starts running about in panic.)* Now don' panic everyone! The police are 'ere! Everyfing's under control! Plane comin' in an' it's on fire! It's on fire! Oh gawd! *(Running up & down.)* Wha' we gonna do, Wilf? Wha' we gonna do?
WILF	Take 'old of tha', Alf. *(Gives him a bucket.)*
ALF	A bucket! Righ'! Righ'! A bucket. OK.
BRIONY	*(Enters.)* Wilf! Have you seen Gertie? I wanted to…
WILF	*(All action.)* No time f'tha' at the moment, Briony. Alf, 'elp me t'bring tha' fire tender over 'ere.
ALF	Righ'! *(They drag it over.)*
BRIONY	But what's the matter?
WILF	Look! *(Points into the sky.)*
BRIONY	What is it?
WILF	Low over the trees! A spitfire… an' it's on fire!

BRIONY	*(Gasps.)* I see it! I see it! Oh! *(Half to herself. Gazing into the sky.)* It's… on… fire! I hope it's not Hugo. Don't let it be Hugo! You see, I did so want to be here for him. The gell back in Blighty. Waiting. Patiently. For him to come home. To be his… comfort. My hand in the air. *(She raises her hand to wave.)* Waving. He… tipping his wings to say he has seen me. *(Pause.)* But… I haven't given him the letter! Oh! Don't let it be…!
GERTIE	*(Enters holding hands with Jack. Very perky.)* Hello everyone! Excitement in abundance rather!
WILF	*(Calm but urgent.)* We in't got time f'nothin' now, Gertie. Stand well back! Come on!
GERTIE	But we've got an announcement!
WILF	It'll just 'ave t' wait a minute, I'm afraid!
GERTIE	*(Miffed.)* But we're… engaged.
BRIONY	*(Shocked.)* Engaged!
WILF	*(Shouting now.)* 'Ere it is! *(Pointing to the sky.)* It's comin' in! *(The noise of the plane's engines are taken up vocally & on the bass. They are all now gripped by the plane's approach.)*
BRIONY	But who is it? Can you see who it is?
WILF	It's… Hugo!
BRIONY	*(She & Gertie gasp.)* Hugo! Oh! *(They cling to each other.)*

ALF   (*Panicking.*) It's comin' in! It's comin' in!

Music 25 – begins.

WILF   Look out! Take cover! It's goin' t' crash! Get be'ind me! Come on!

Hugo flies in, struggling to control the plane as it shudders to a halt in front of them. A mimed sequence begins with them first taking avoiding action & then heroically putting out the flames. They pull out the fire tender, point the hose at the 'flames', pass buckets along a line and as a group lift the unconscious Hugo from the cockpit and carry him overhead to a bench DSL. They reel as the plane explodes again. All'improvviso: 'Look out! Watch out f'the fuel tank! It's going to explode! Wilf! Come back! Mind yuhself, Gertie! Get his legs, Briony! Steady! Steady. Take 'im over there. Mind your feet. Careful! Careful! Etc.'

Music 25 – ends.

BRIONY   Hugo! Hugo! (*All'improvviso from the others. 'He's coming round! Is he alright? Give him some air. Etc, etc.'*)
HUGO   (*After a moment.*) I say, you cheps! Bravo rather!
GERTIE   He's alright! He's alright! (*All'improvviso: Bravo! Well done all of you! Well done everyone! You were all so brave! Etc.' They all clap & hug.*)

BRIONY	Oh, Hugo! You're safe! I was so so worried about you! *(Runs to him & hugs him. He accepts the embrace but is a little restrained. She pulls away embarrassed.)*
ALF	Well you gave us a bit of a scare there, young man! Still, it were all under control! No panic! No panic at all!
GERTIE	*(They all laugh.)* Course not, PC Wood! Not with the local constabulary in charge!
JACK	Well, I think all you cheps were very brave! Especially Wilf! Three cheers for Wilf! *(They give three cheers. All'improvviso: 'Wilf! Wilf! Etc.')*
WILF	An' wha' was it I 'eard in all the kafuffle? Tha' certain people 'ave got engaged! Well, tha's a surprise! *(All'improvviso: 'Well done you two! Congratulations! Etc.' Briony conspicuously turns away for a moment.)*
GERTIE	You see, Briony. We are so very happy!
BRIONY	*(Stalwart, then after a brief pause.)* Yes, I believe you are. Well done chum!
JACK	Well! What d'yuh say, you cheps? Down the pub, ay? Pork scratchings on me! *(All'mprovviso. 'Yes! Rather! Not half! Etc.')*

Jack & Gertie exit entwined. Alf follows them, but Will hovers at a distance, concerned.

BRIONY	*(Suddenly remembering.)* Oh, Hugo! I've just remembered. There was a letter for you. Mrs Beeskep asked me to give it to you. Here it is. (*She takes it out & gives it to him.*)
HUGO	I say, a letter! How perfectly splendid! *(Rips it open & reads.)* It's from... *(Looks at Briony)* Terri.
BRIONY	Terri? Oh.
HUGO	Teresa... My wife.

Music 26 – begins.

> *Briony turns sharply away. Desolate.*

	She says little Bertie is having a terrific time at school. Settled in really well. Nort missing home at all. Hugo junior has been promoted to the first team at cricket end... the twins are growing bigger every day. *(Slight pause. Restrained.)* Splendid.
BRIONY	*(Swings round.)* How marvellous! How ebsolutely... marvellous. What a... lovely... *big*... family you have. *(Turns away again. He looks at her for a moment, his hand hovering over her arm, then exits.)*

Music 26 – ends.

WILF	*(Comes forward.)* All right there, Briony?
BRIONY	Yes, thenk you.
WILF	*(Comes forward. Pause.)* Want me t'walk you 'ome? I c'n go your way.
BRIONY	*(Turning round to him.)* No thenk you, but thet's very kind. You *are*... a very kind chep, Wilf.
WILF	*(Pause.)* Jus' though' you might like... a bit a company, like. *(Pause.)* There's always another day, y'know, Briony. Every day brings somethin' new. 'Specially in times like these. You know tha', don'cha? New folks. New... lads.
BRIONY	*(Recovers. Smiling.)* Yes! Another day. Always something new! Maybe I'll join the WI! Make myself useful! Or the lend army. Thet'll be fun.
WILF	The land army! Tha's a good idea. All the gerls are joinin' up. *(Pause.)* See yuh then. *(Exits. She waits for a moment, despondent. Then pulls herself together, takes a deep breath & exits jauntily a different way.)*

Music 27 – begins & ends.

GEORGE	*(Enters. He has a fork & starts digging up cabbages.)* Lil! 'Ow abou' a cuppa tea an' some a'tha' upside down cake? *(To the audience. Shows them a cabbage.)*

	Look at tha'! Tha's a beaut, innit? Cabbages for a king!
LIL	There you are then! Cuppa tea an' a piece of cake. An' don't say I don' do nothin' for yuh. *(He takes it.)* Now, yuh should've heard what Alf was sayin' about Wilf! A proper hero, 'e said! Gettin' up there on tha' aeroplane when it were covered in flames an' all, an' draggin' tha' young pilot t'safety. I wouldn' be surprised if 'e don' get a medal.
GEORGE	Yes. 'E's a good lad. *(Nightshade flies in with a ring in his mouth & starts playing with it.)*
LIL	An' Jack an' Alf an' the girls! They all did their bit by all accounts. So Alf say. Heroes! All of 'em! Tha's wha' I think!
GEORGE	Tha's righ'. It makes yuh proud! Ay! Look at tha' magpie. Wha's 'e got'? 'E's got sommat. *(To Nightshade.)* 'Ere! Shoo! Gimme tha'! *(Tries to shoo him away, but he resists & holds on to the ring.)*

Yewberry & Thorn fly in and harass George.

LIL	Look out!
GEORGE	Jeez! *(Takes avoiding action.)* Vicious li'le buggers in't they! Go on! Shoo! *(They fly off & George picks up the ring.*

	The magpies gather again a little way off.) It's a ring! Look at tha'! Well, I'll be! *An'* it looks silver t' me. I wonder where they got it from. *(Studies it closely.)*
LIL	They all got their funny li'le ways. Birds. Magpies is jus' a bi' greedy, tha's all. Personally, with all this 'Itler stuff goin' arf an' the young men goin' t'war, the one thing I like t'do is listen t'the birds with their innocent li'le twi'erin'. It's lovely! Tha's wha' I think. *(To the birds.)* Come on! Birdies! Come on! 'Ave a bi' of my upside down cake! *(She throws them some crumbs.)*

The magpies simultaneously take a drag on cigarettes & scowl at the audience.

MAGPIES	Kark!

Music 28 – begins & ends.

BOWS